This Book

Belongs To

....

....

....

....

I0408006

Relaxation

Coloring Book for Adults

OANCEA CAMELIA

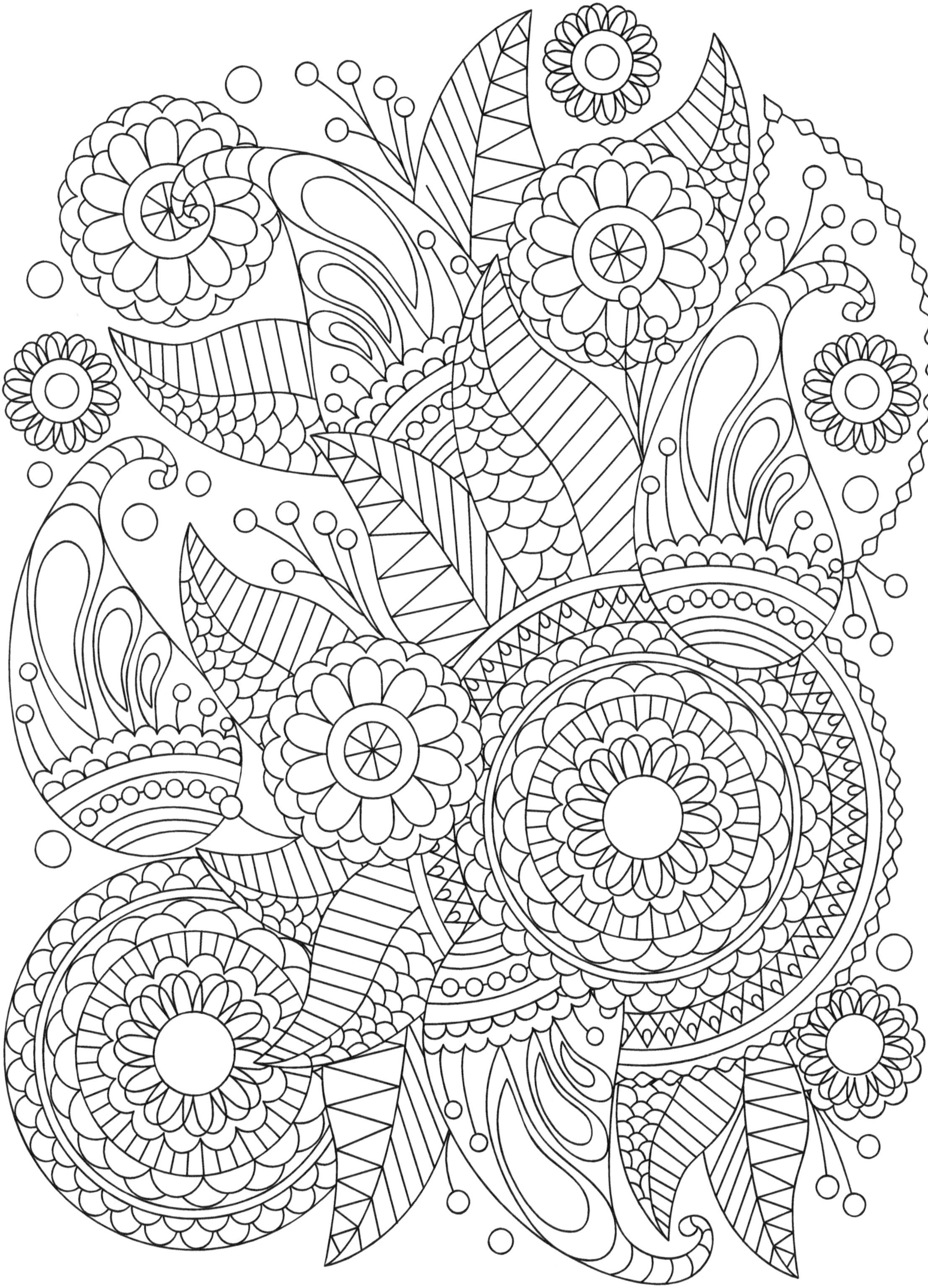

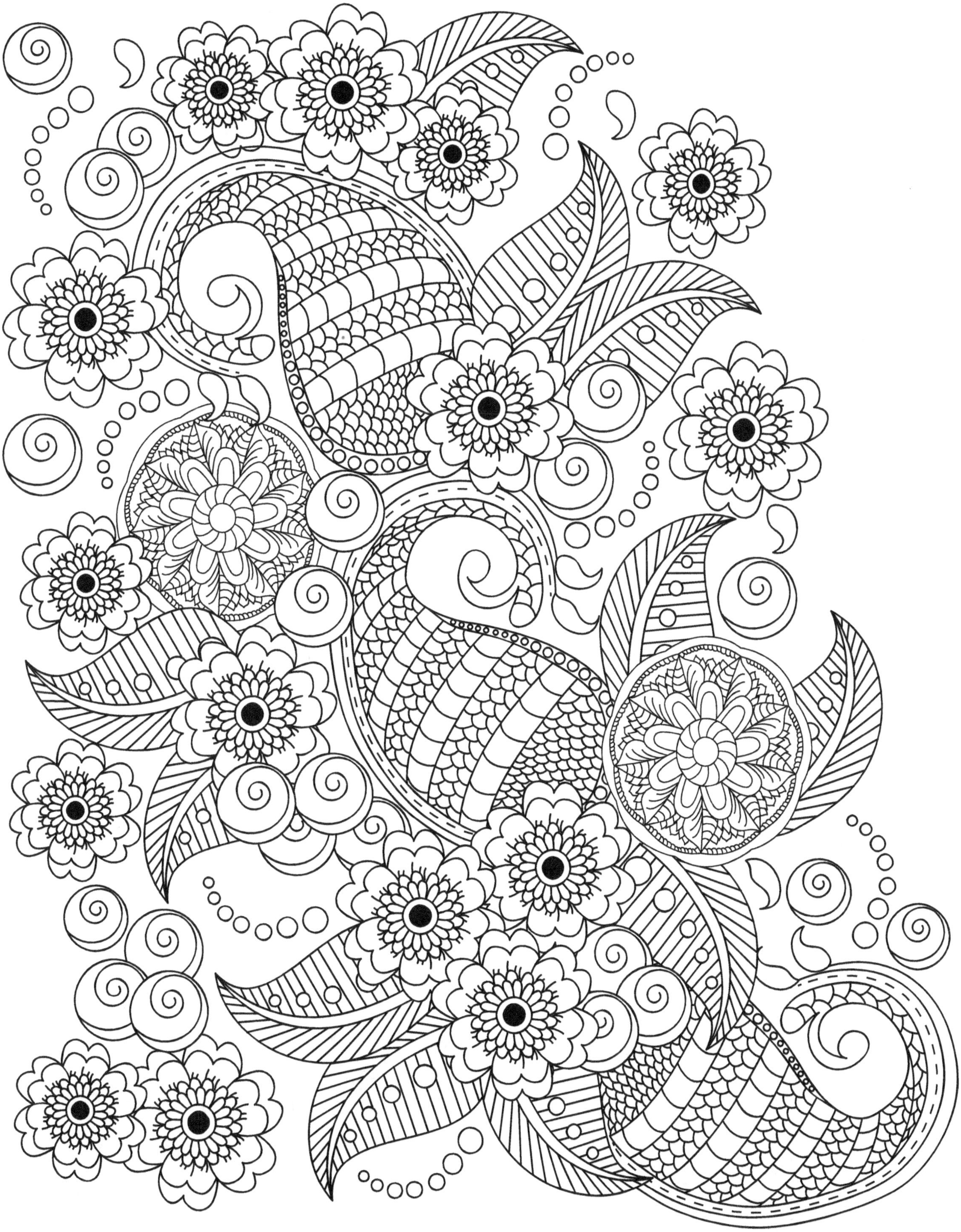

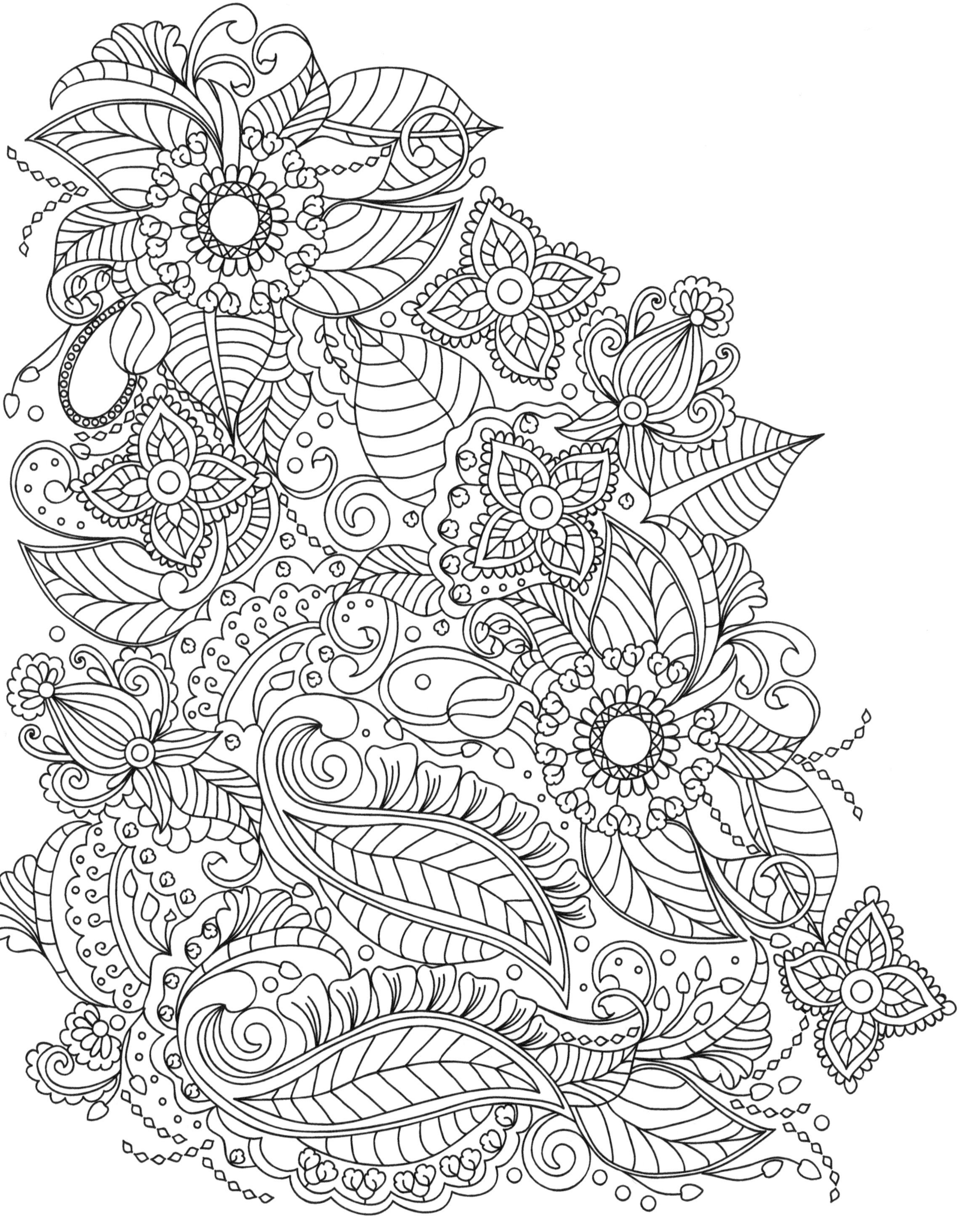

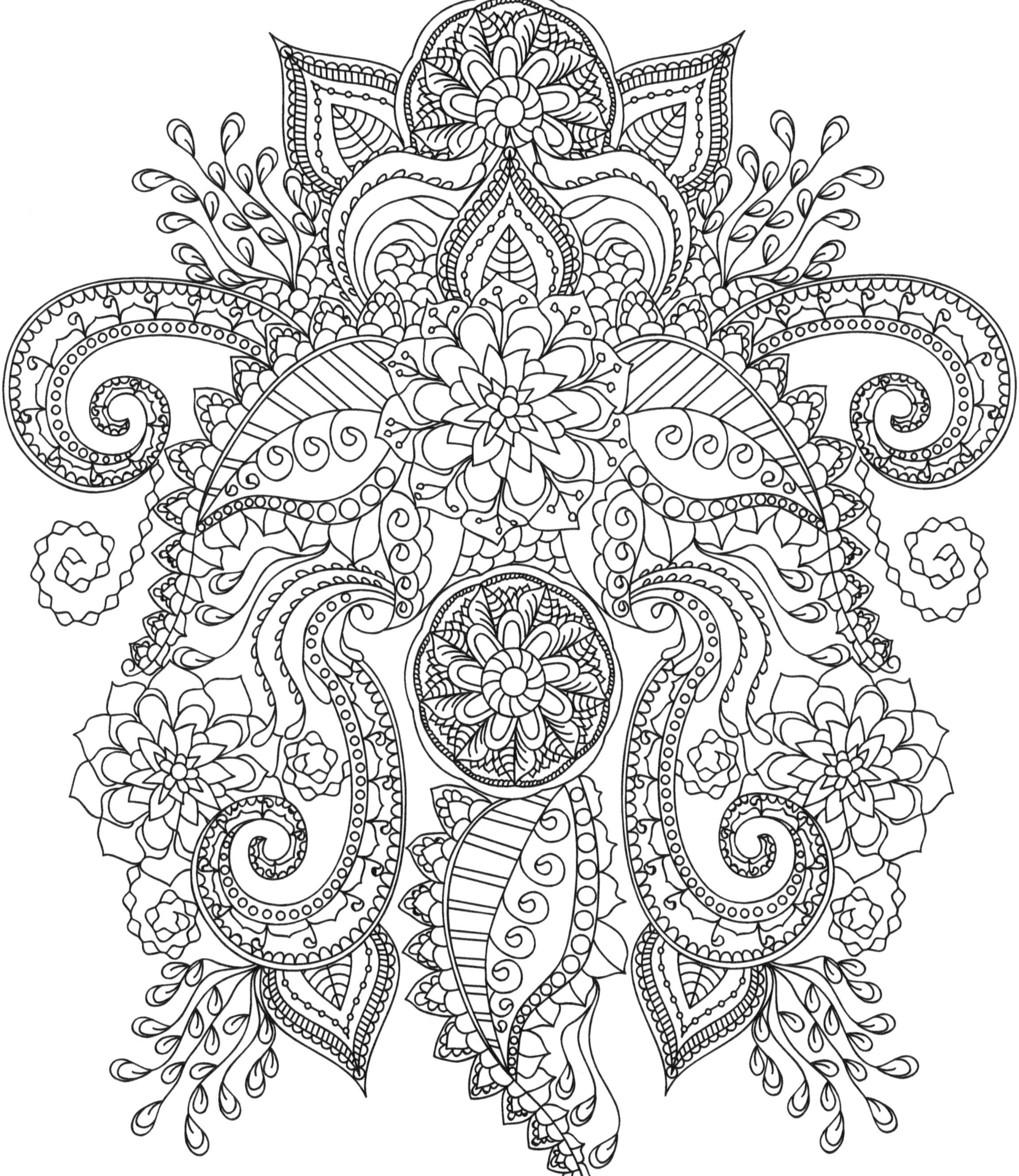

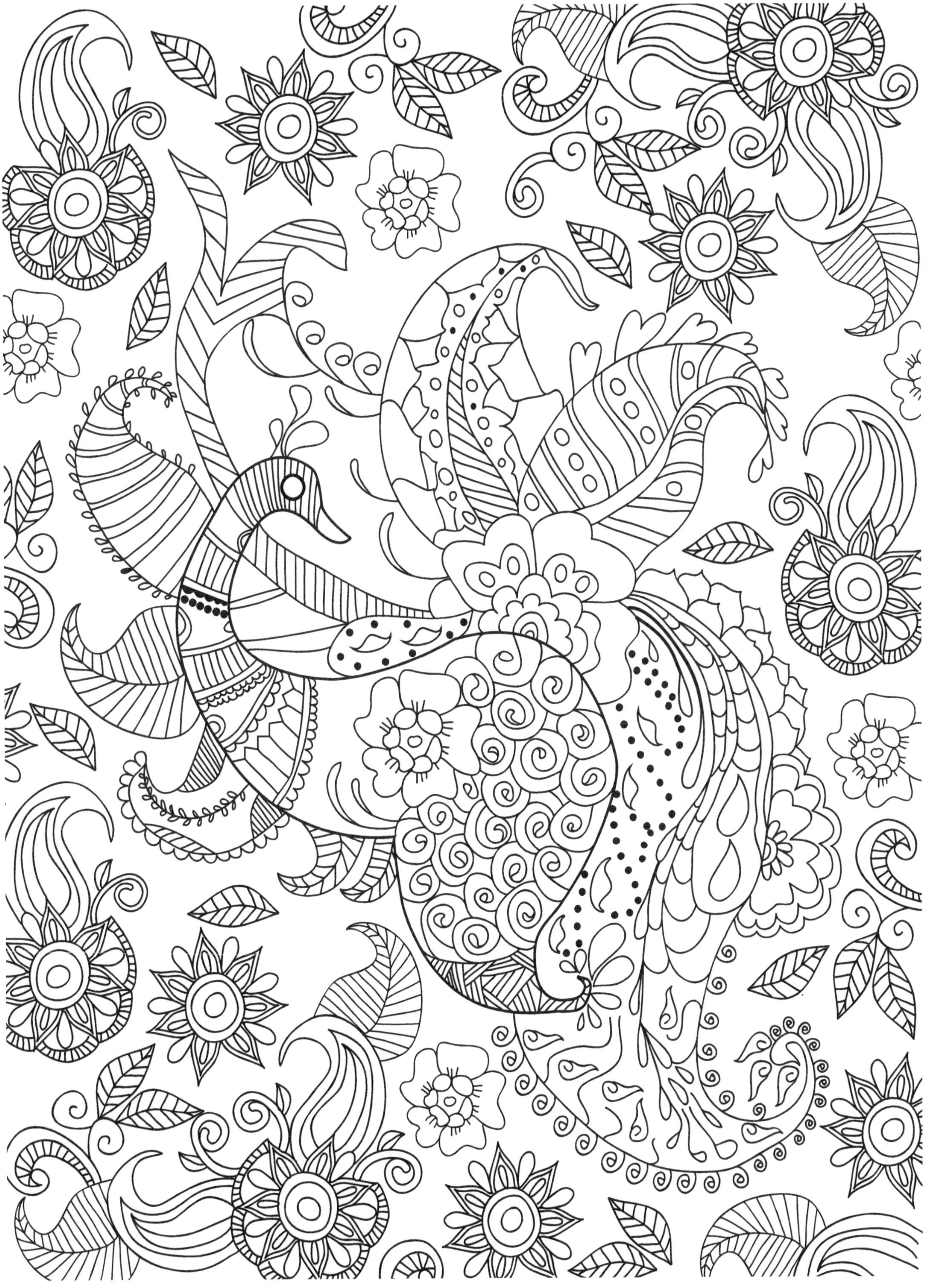

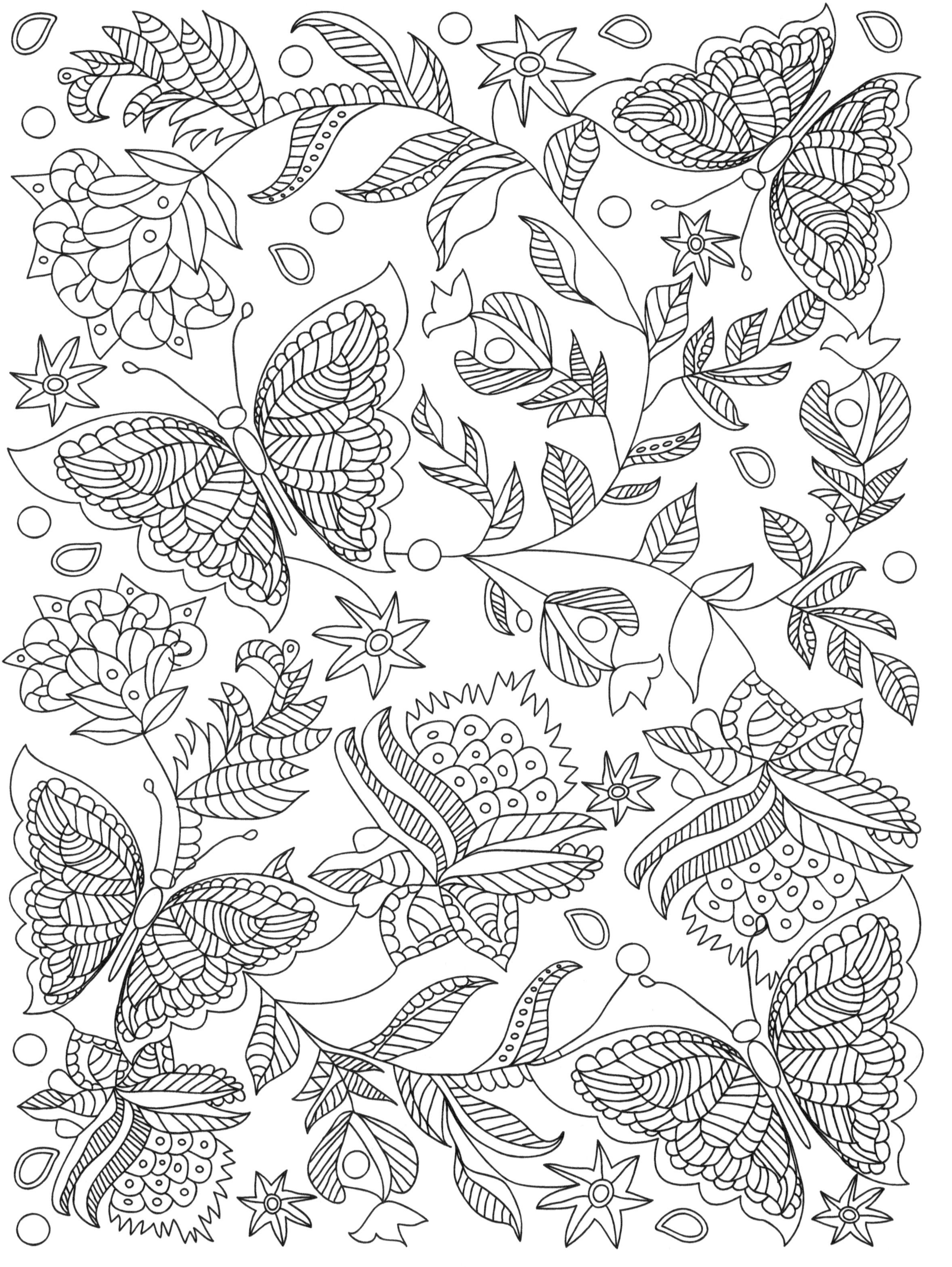

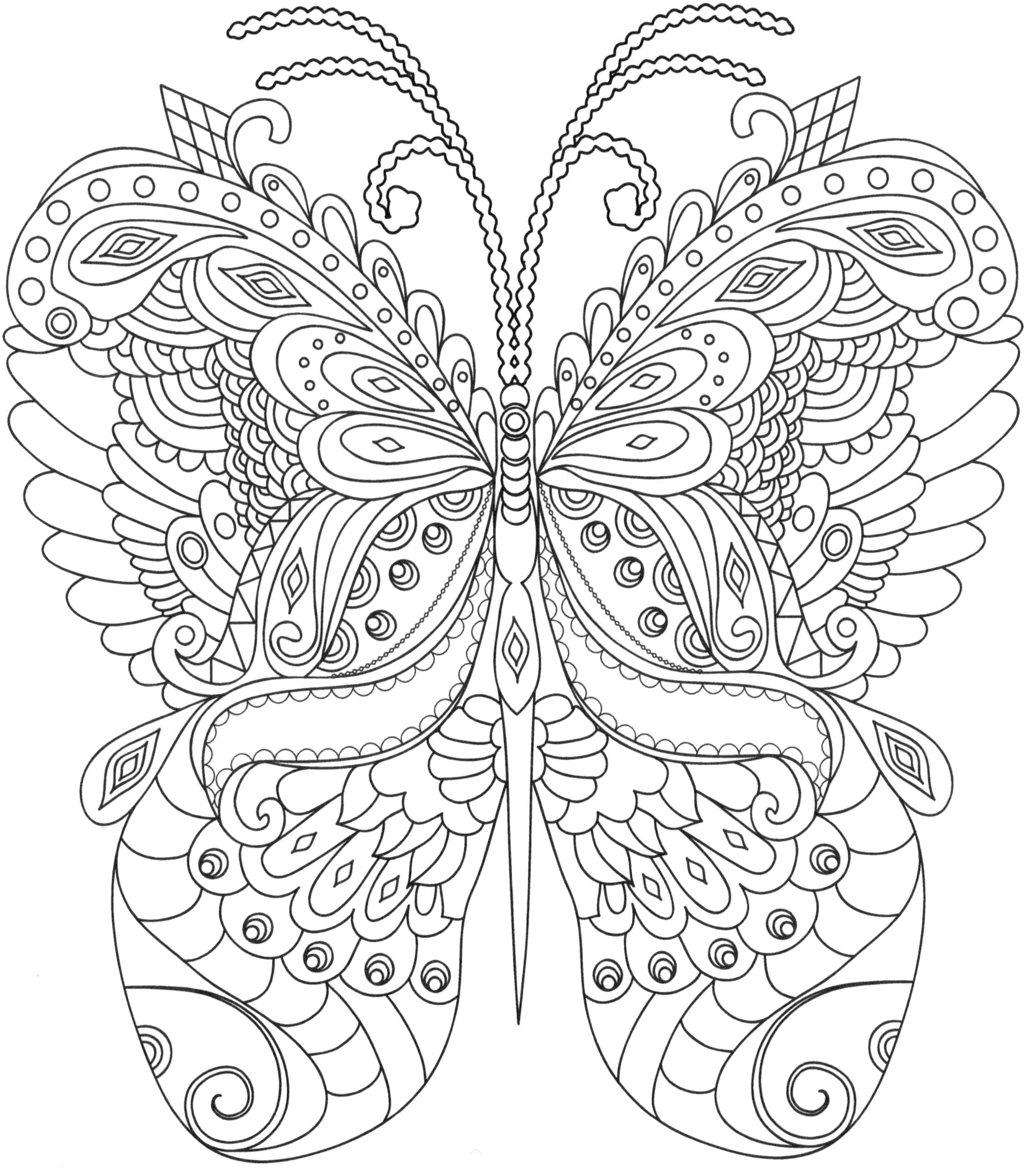

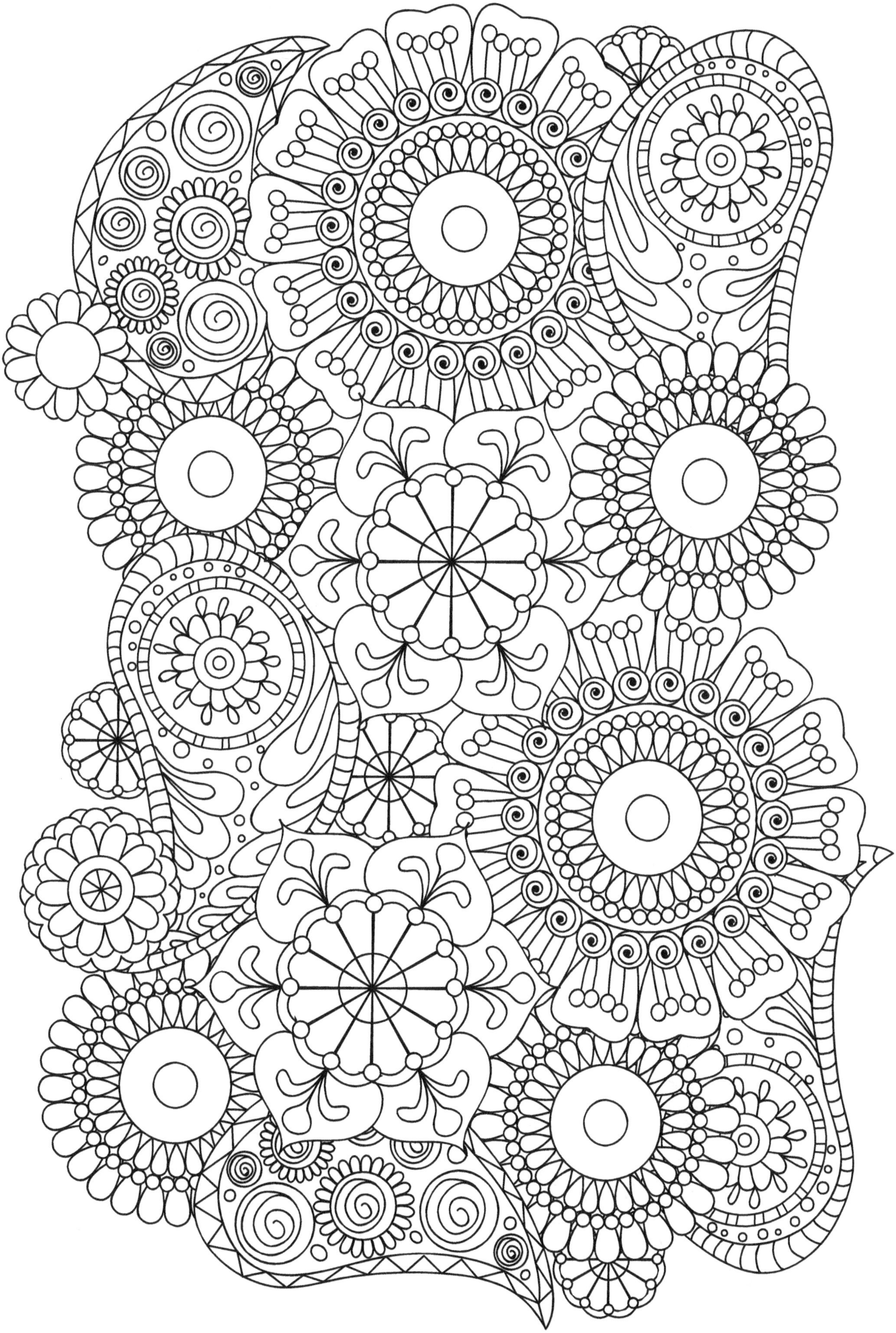

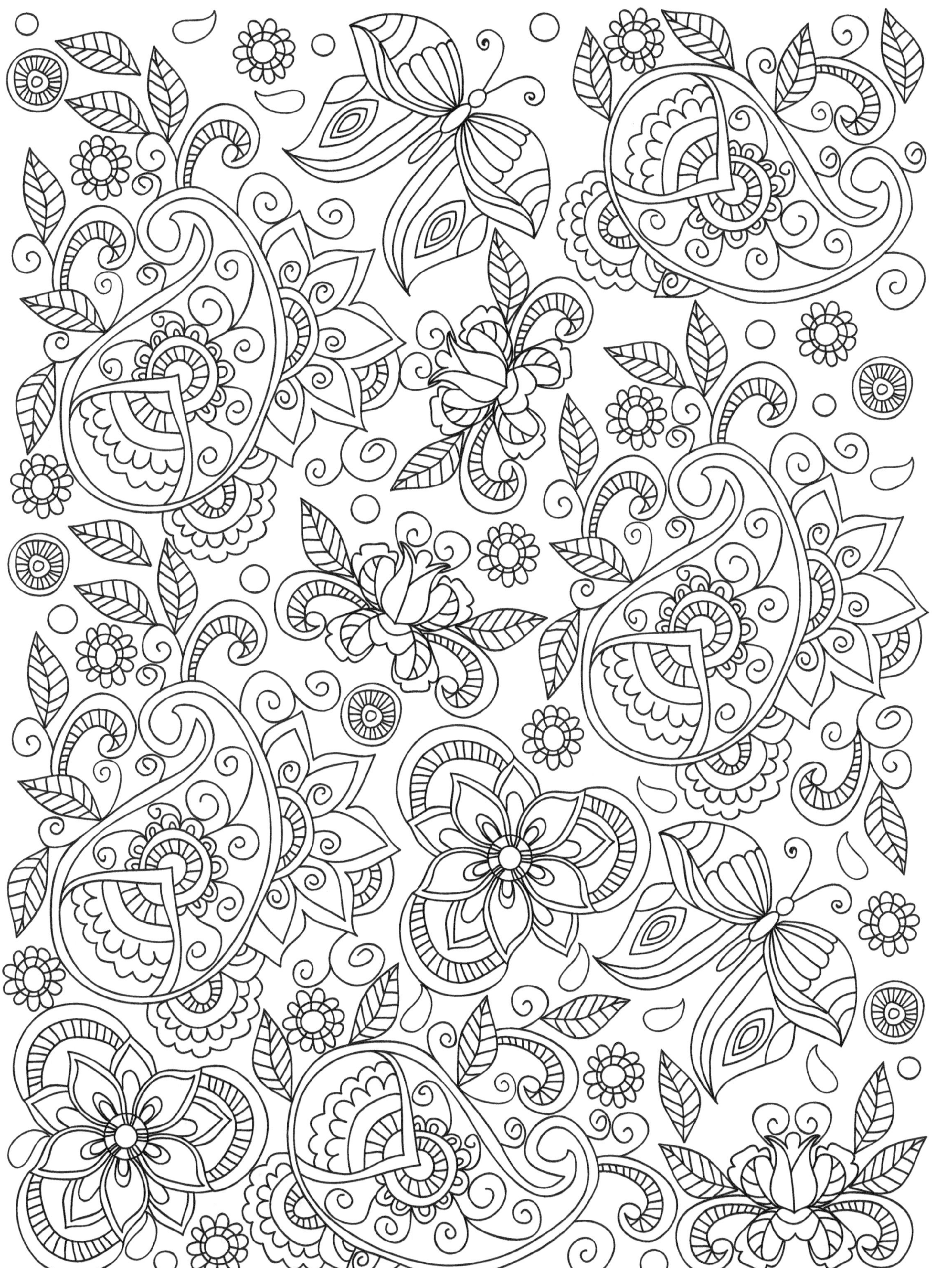

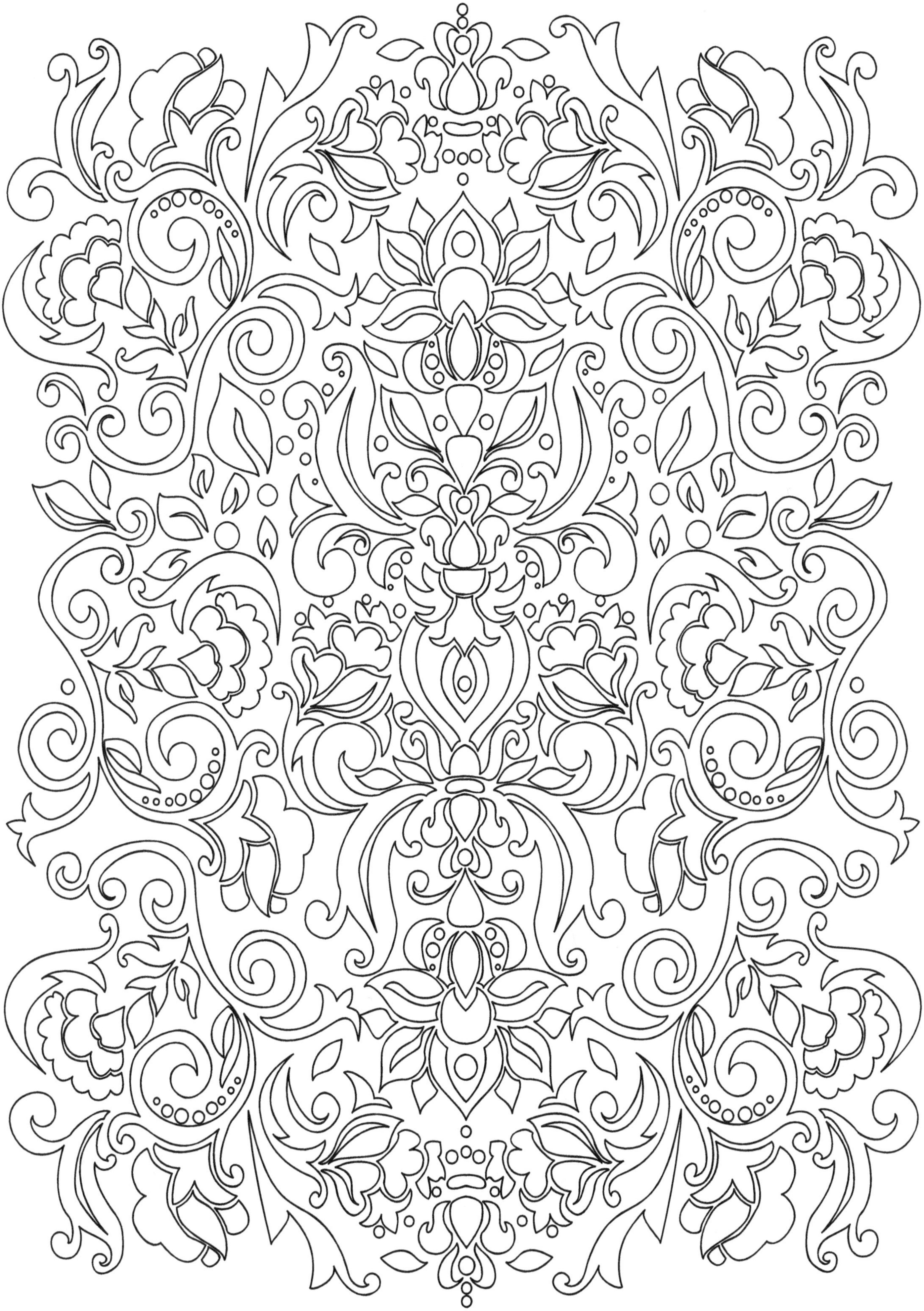

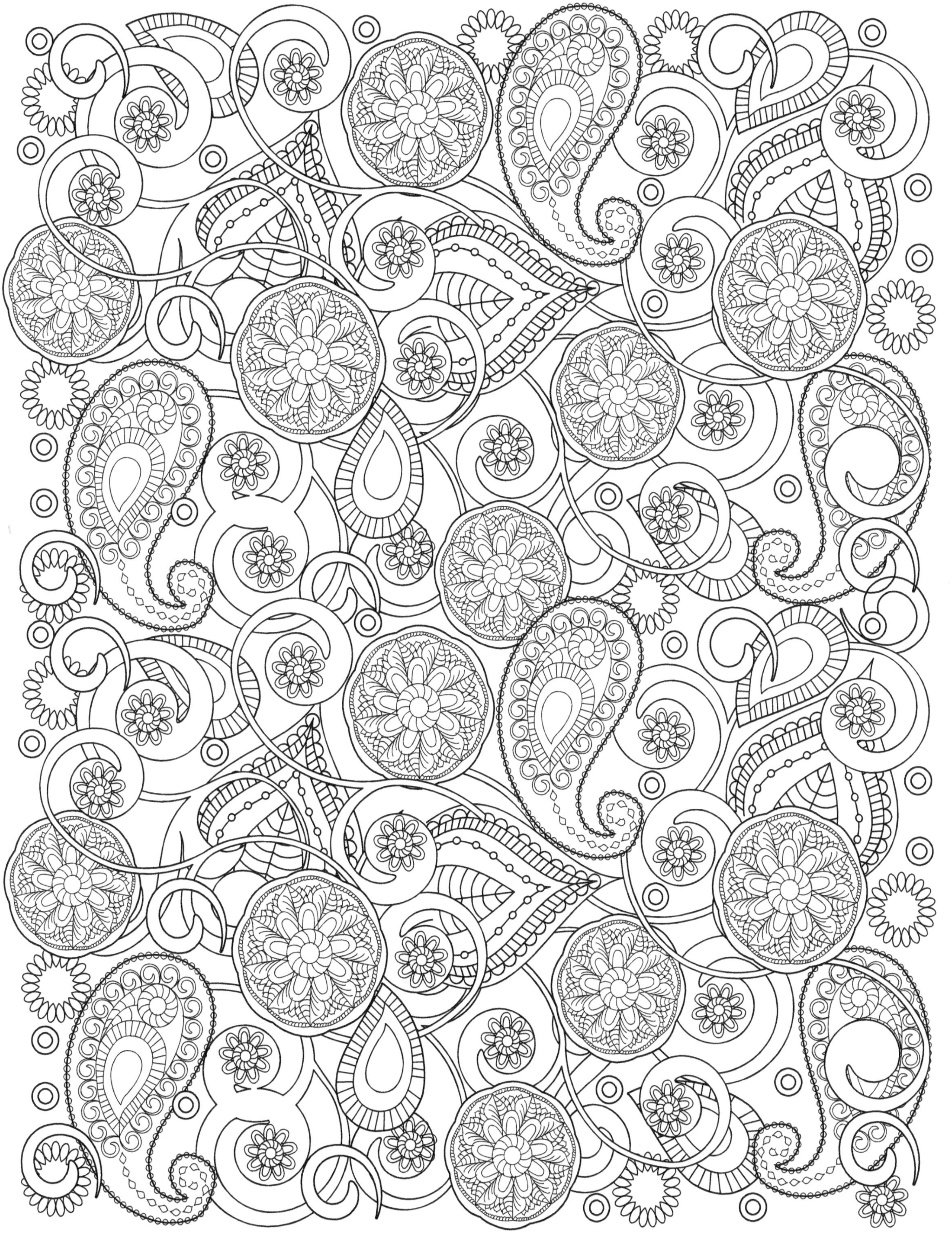

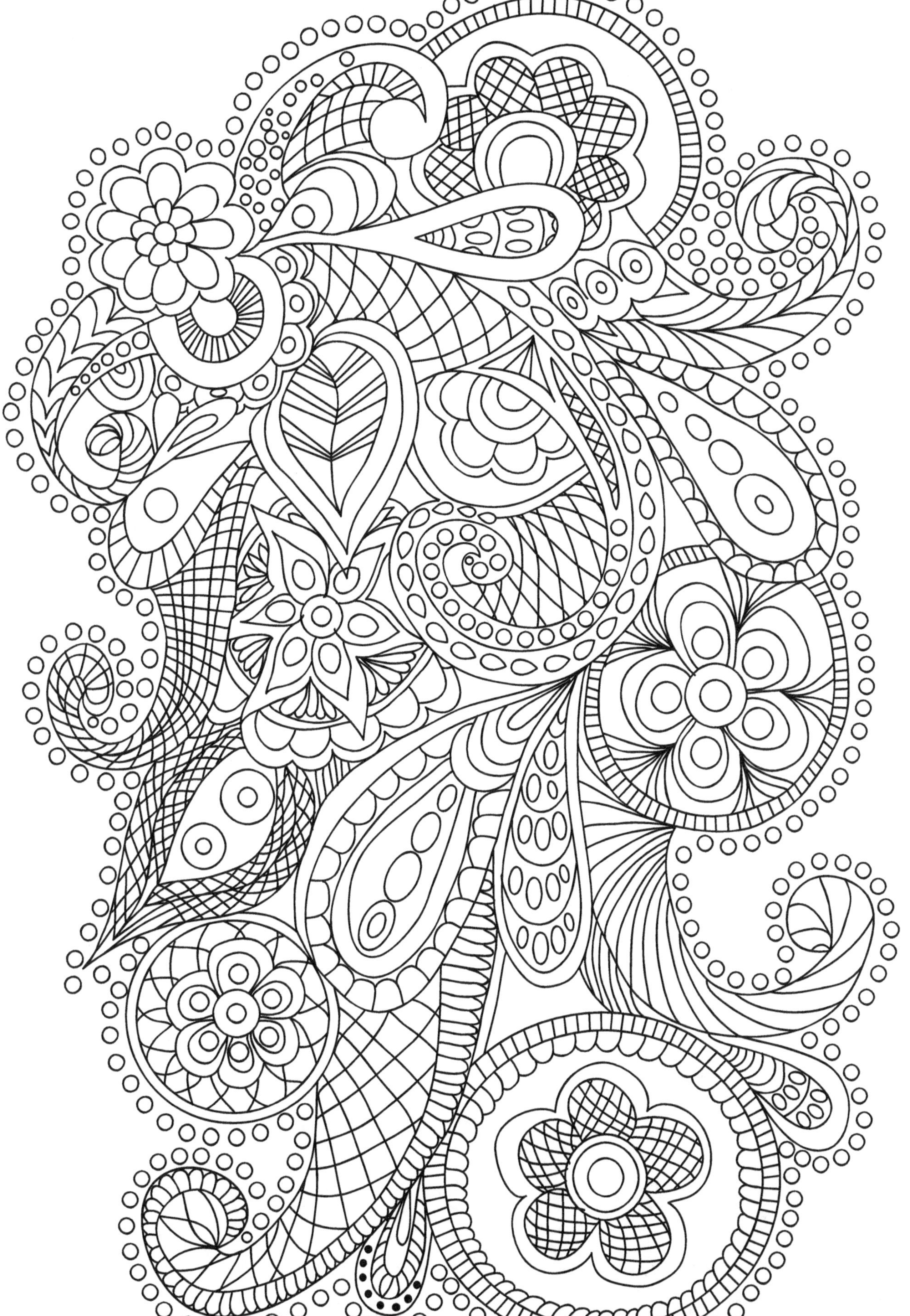

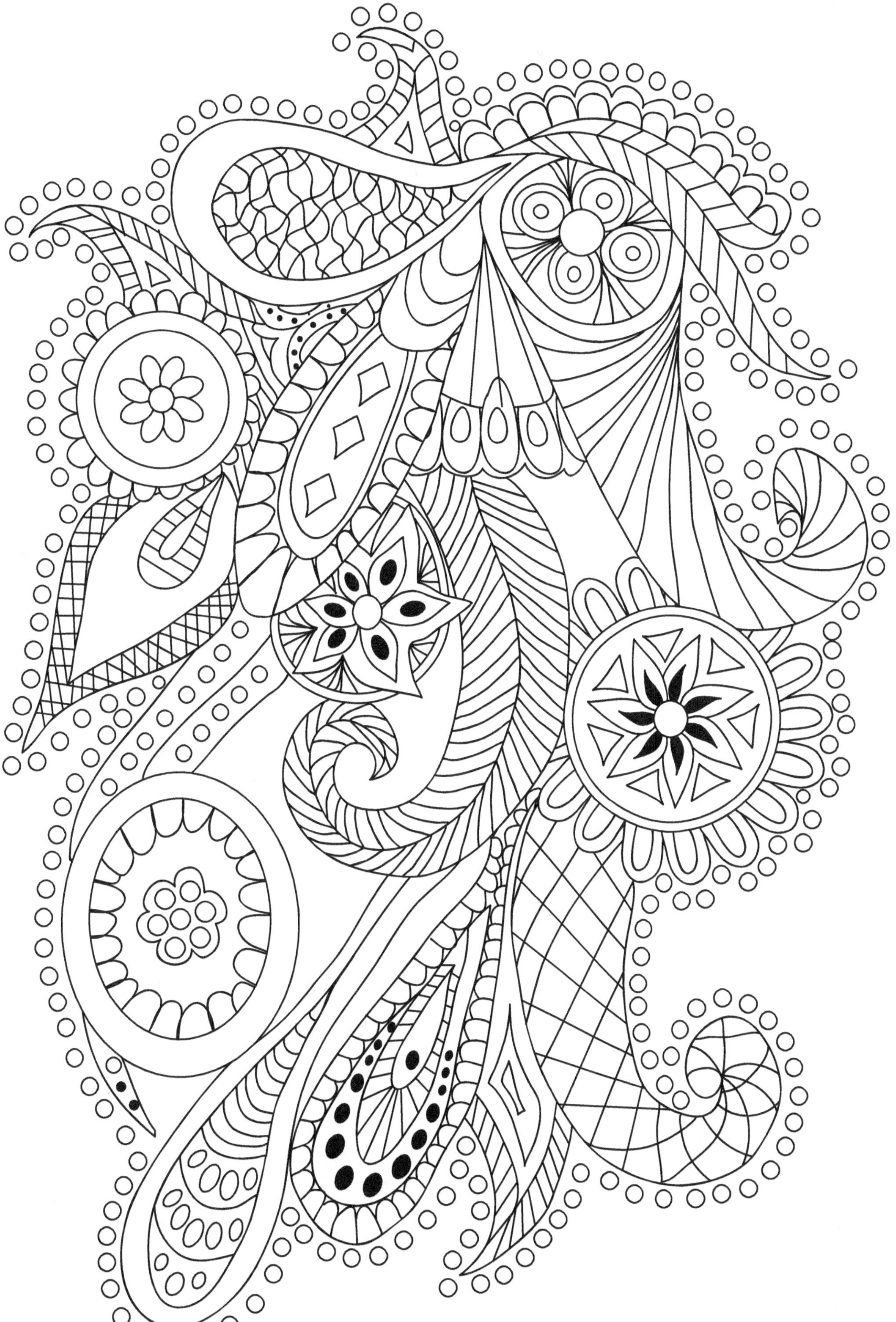

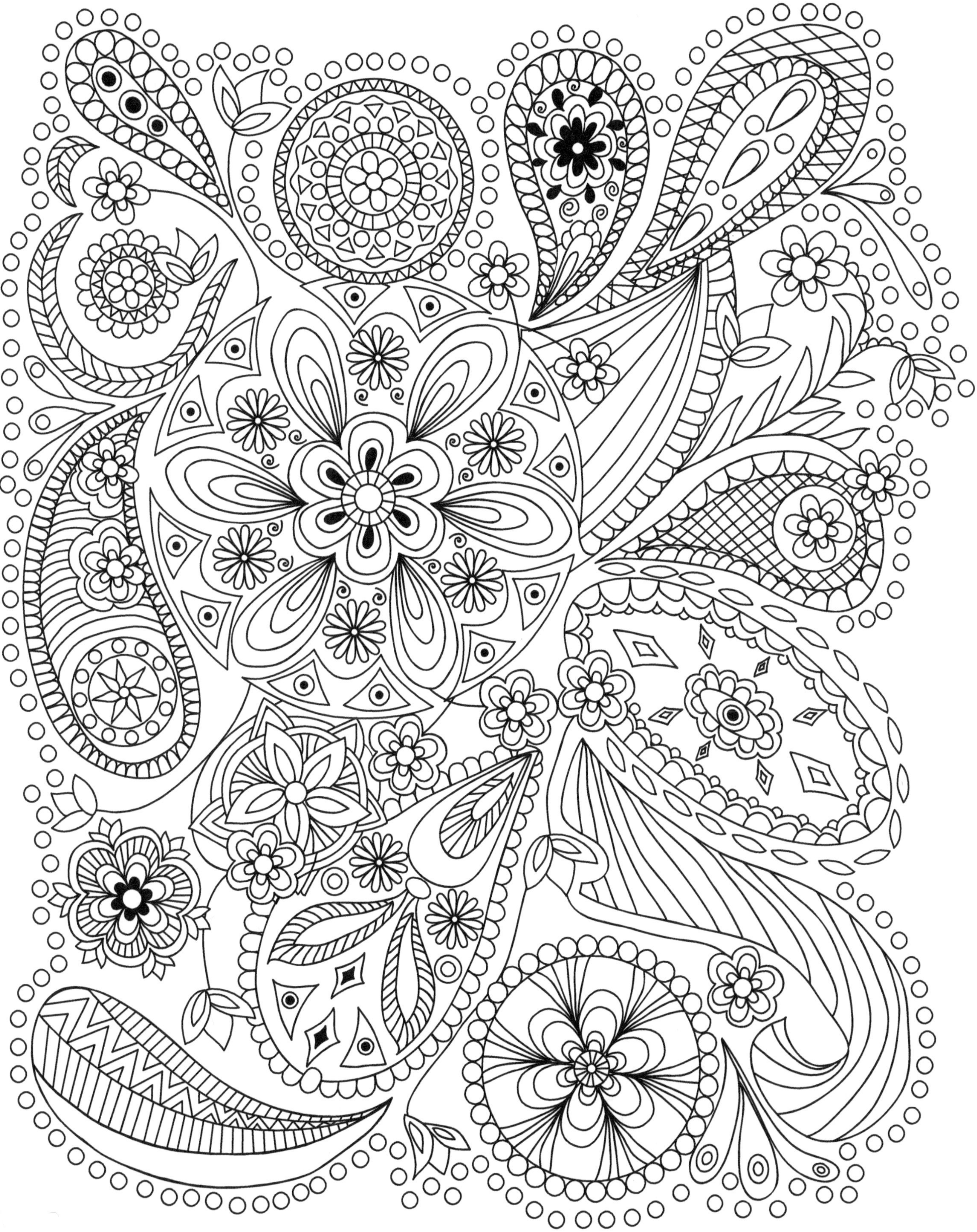

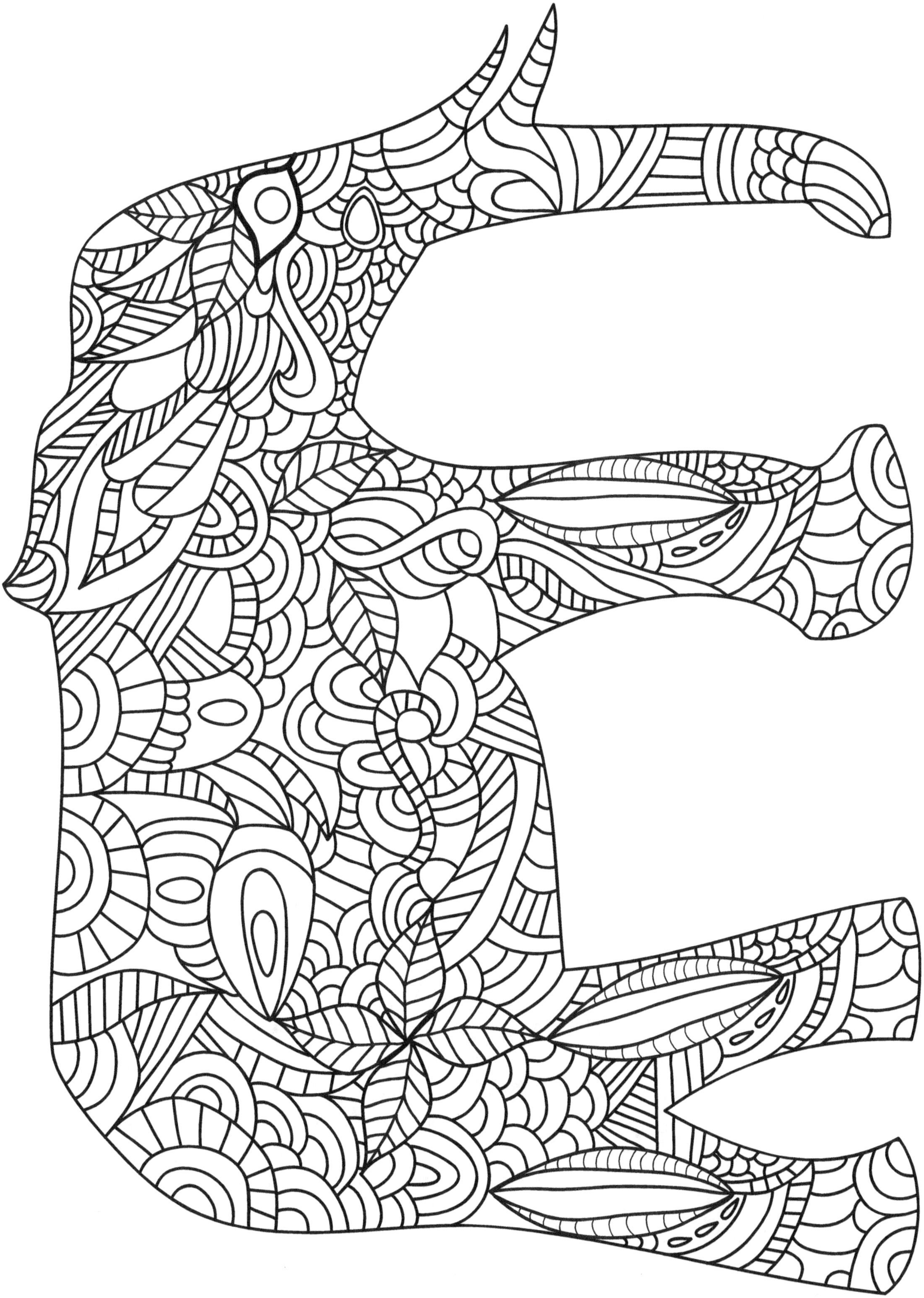

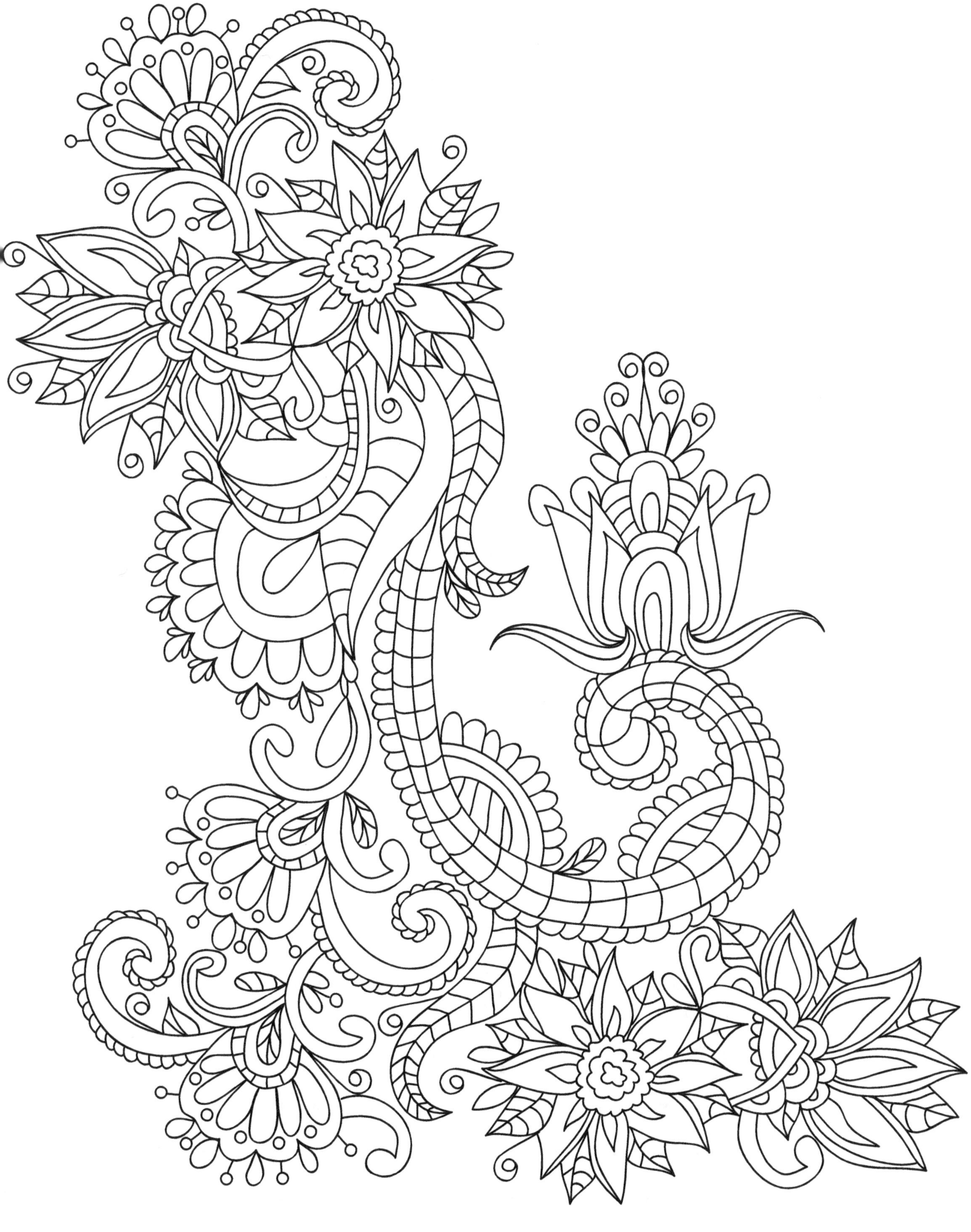

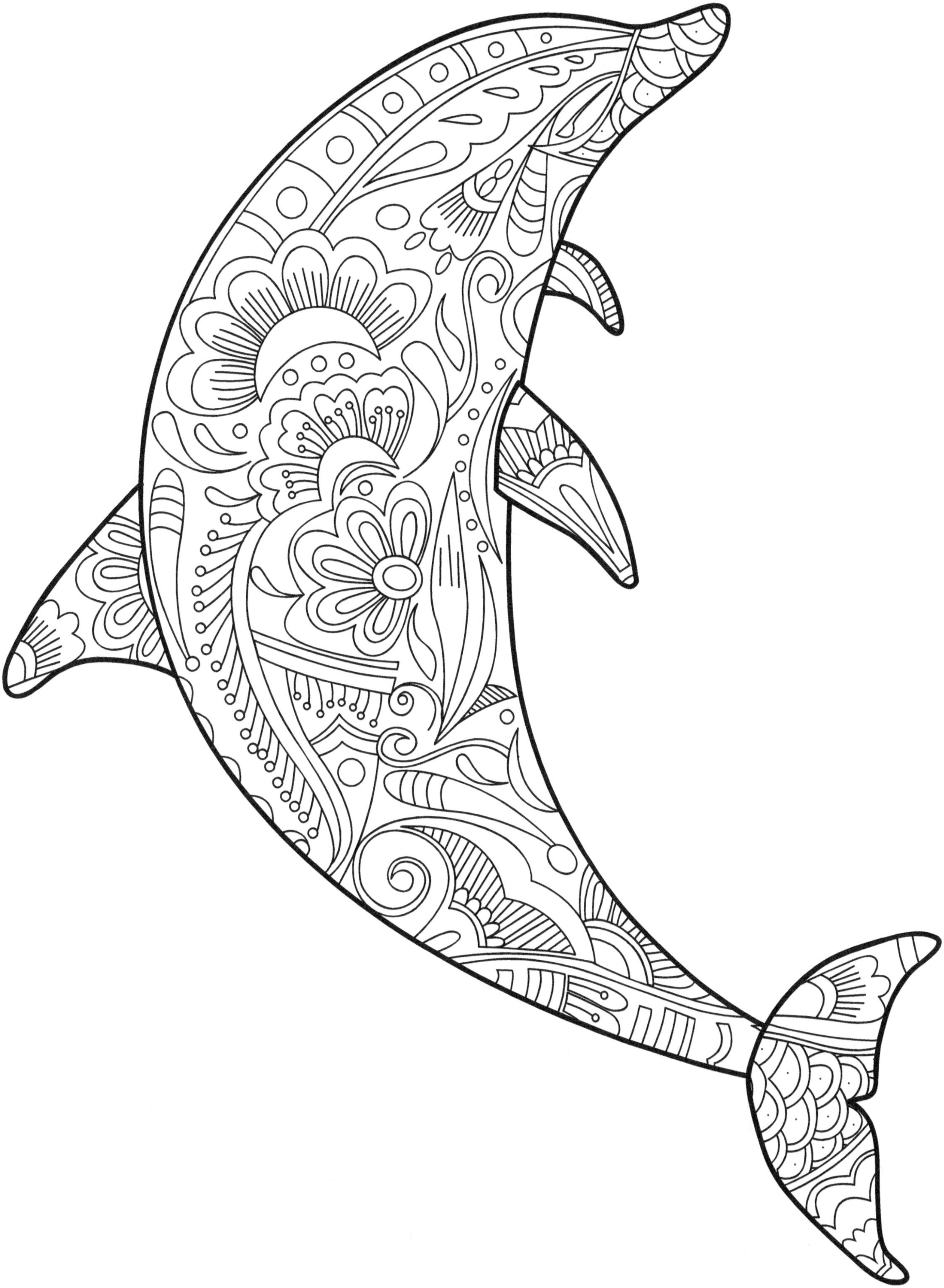

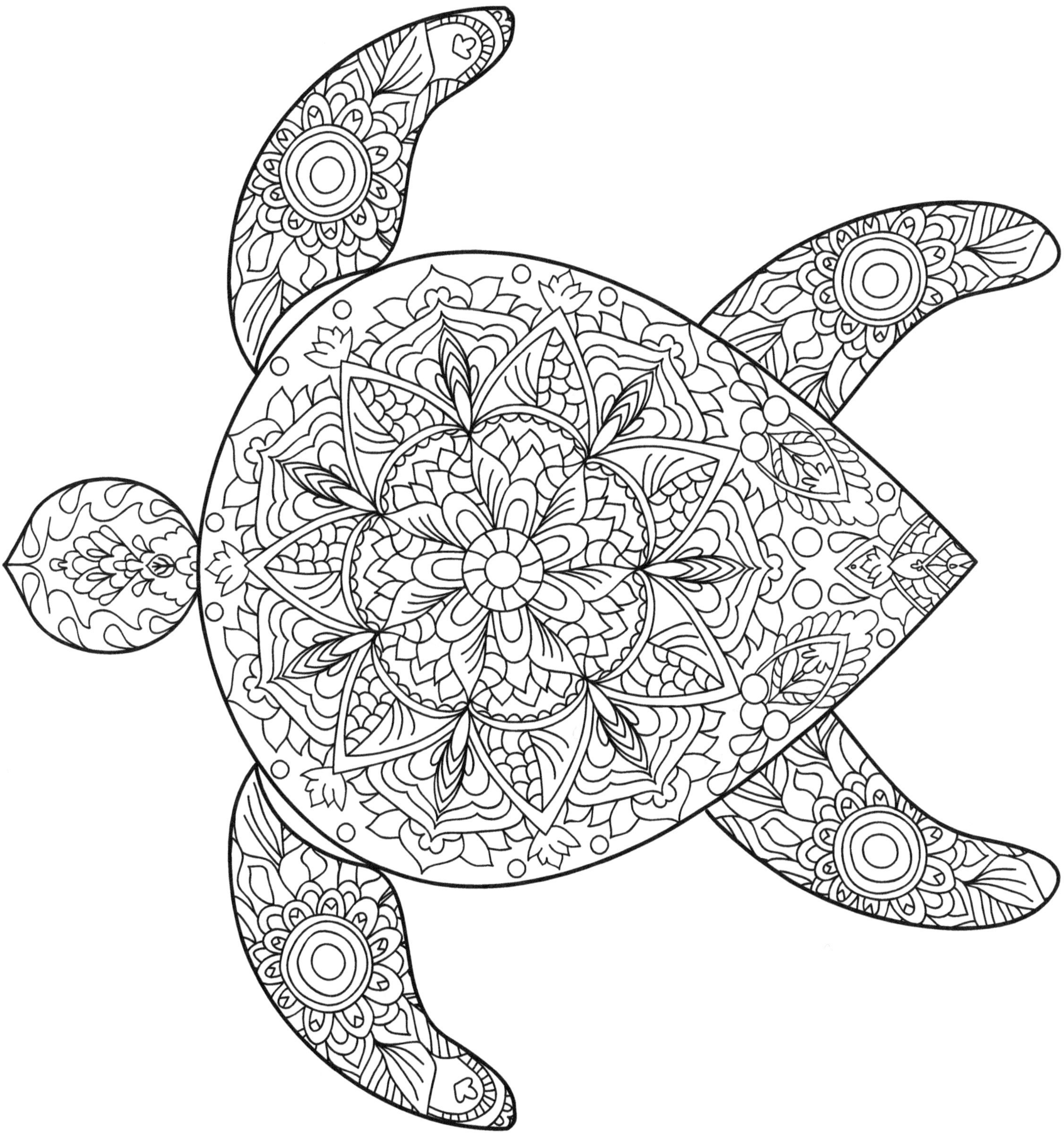

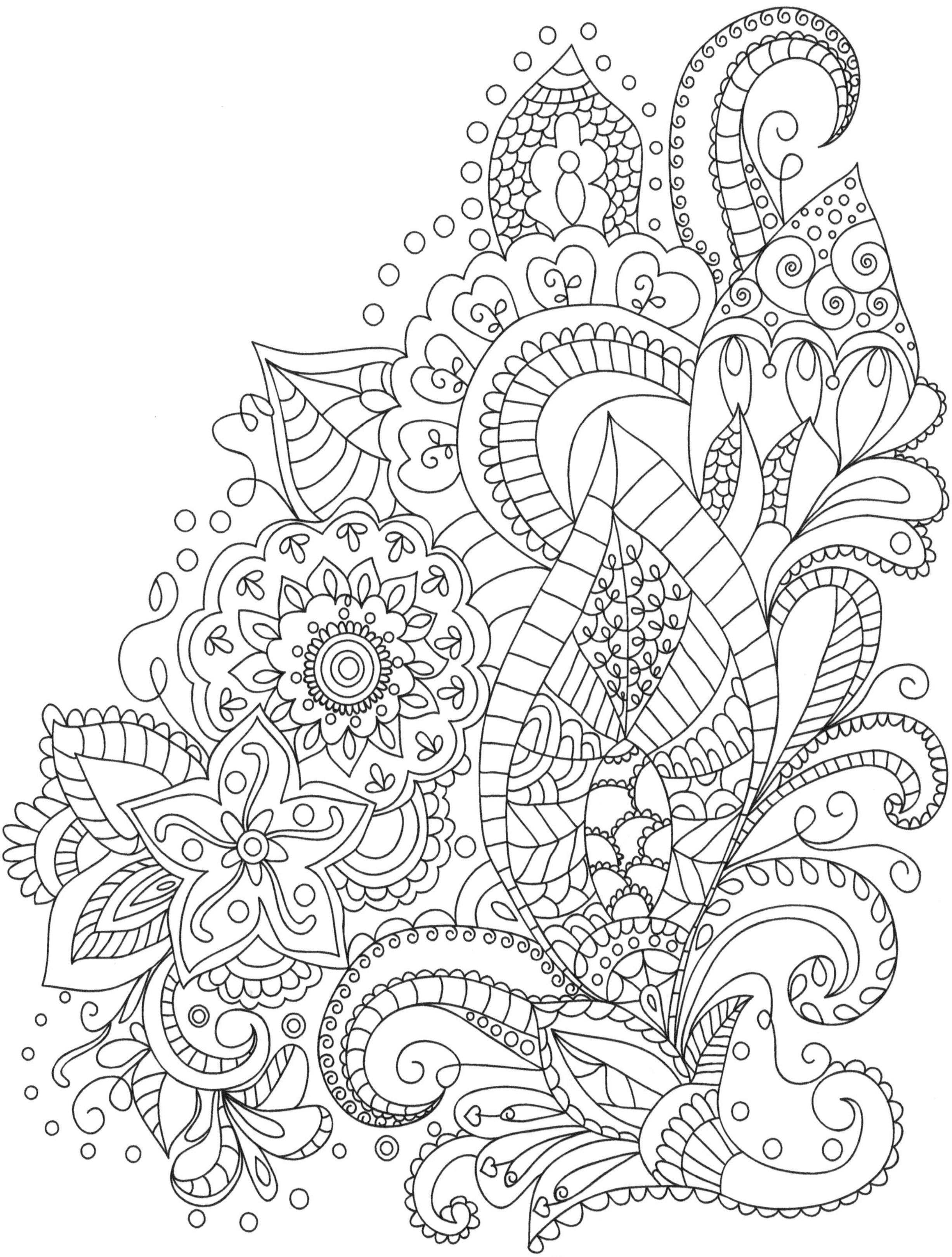

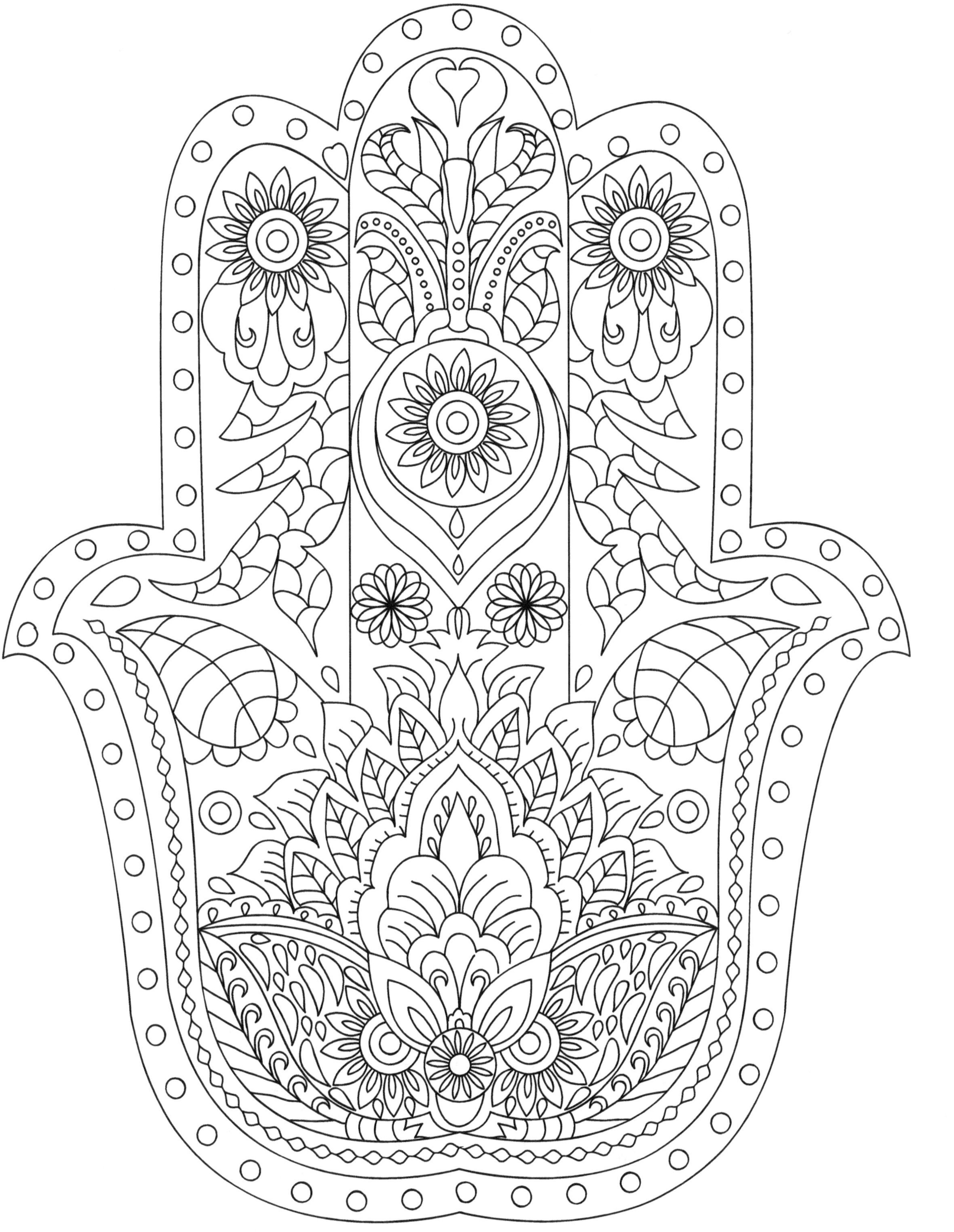

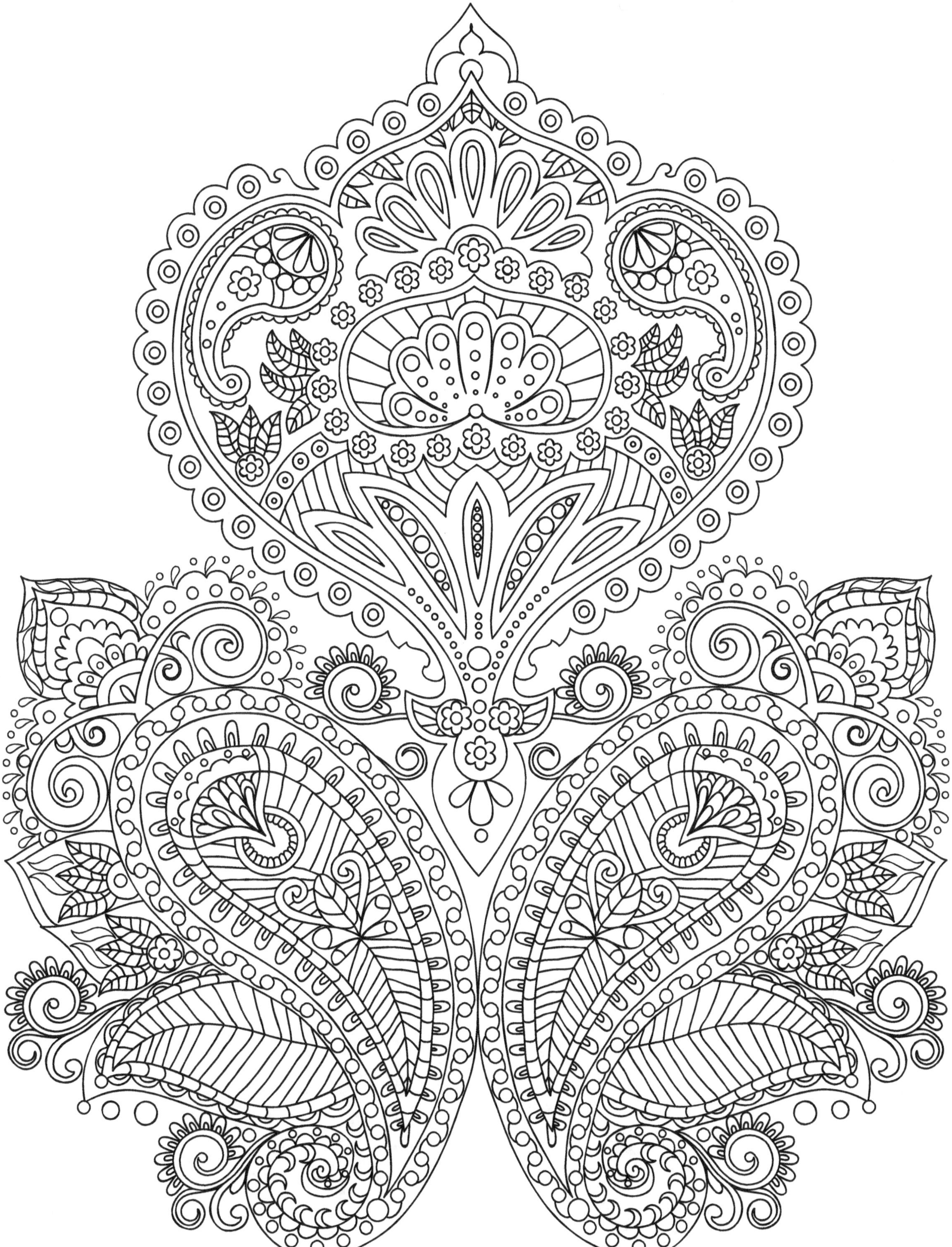

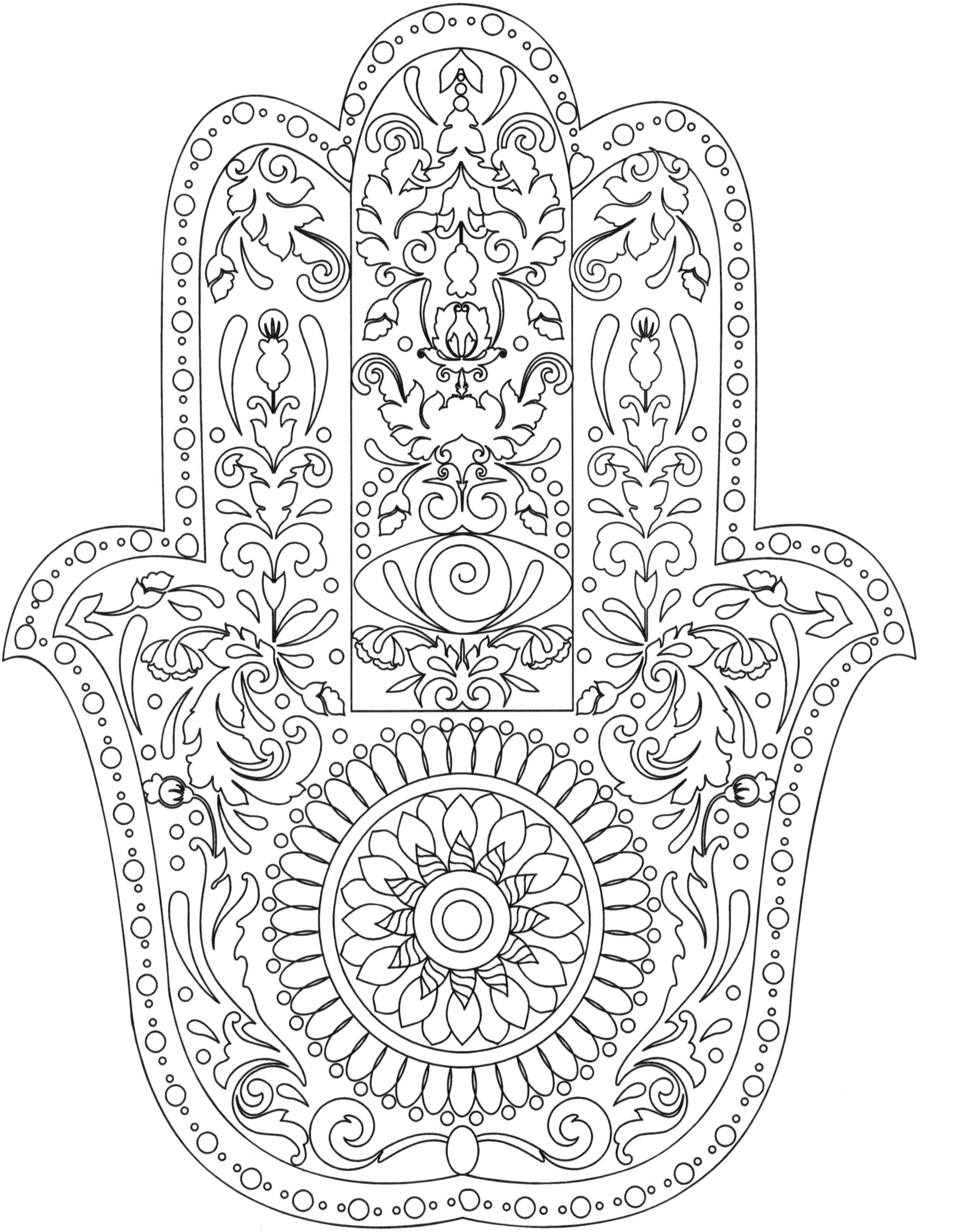

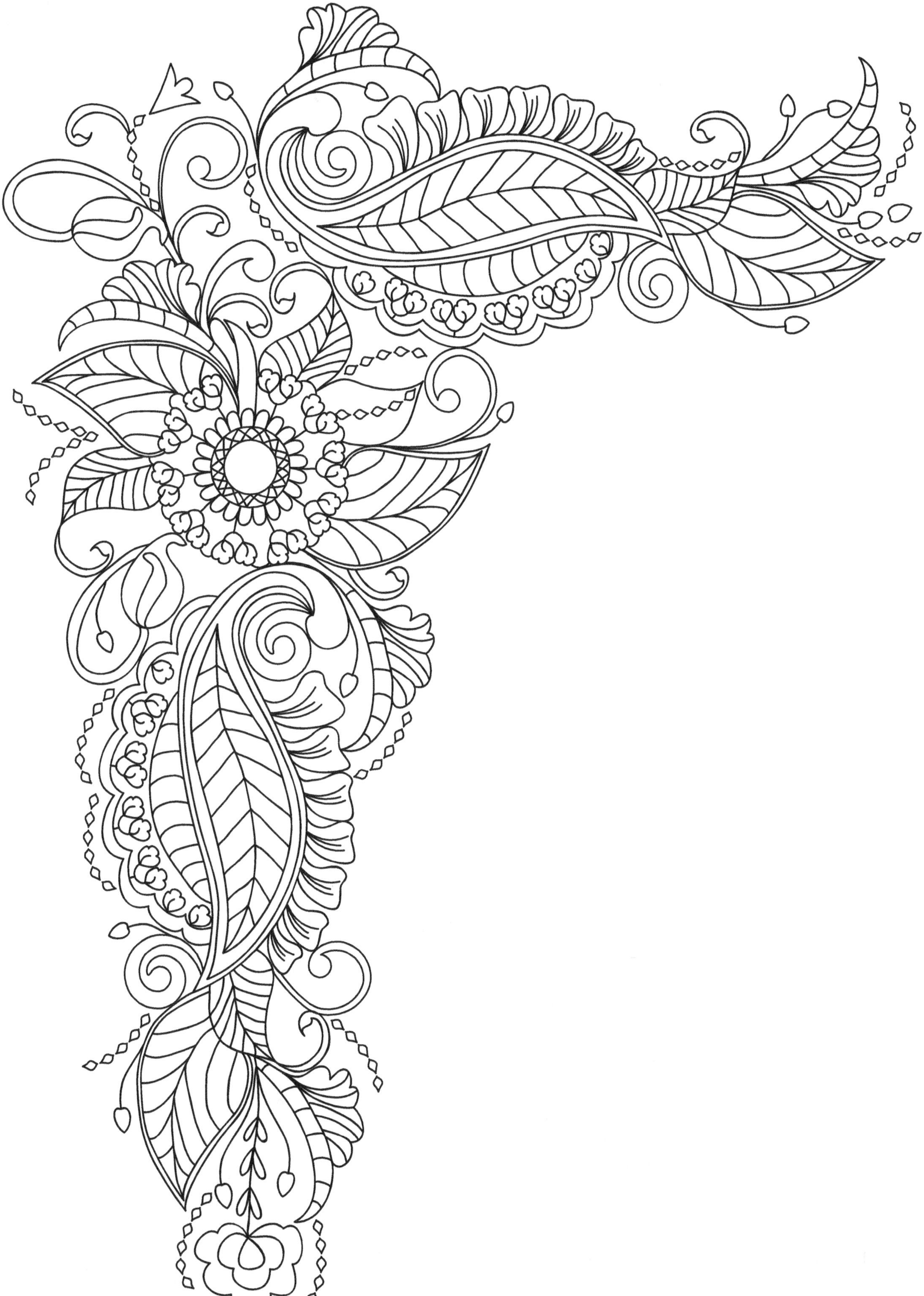

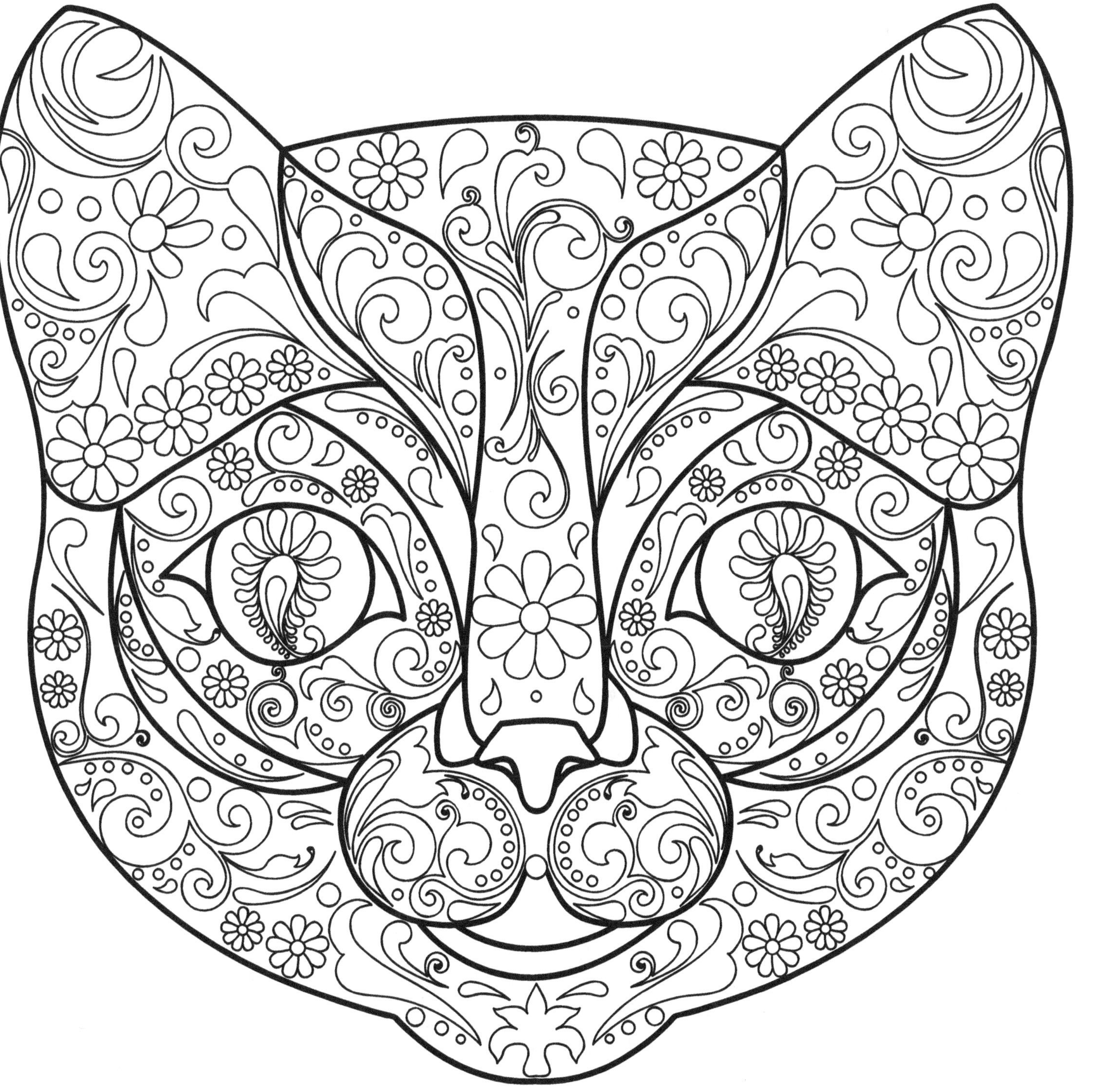

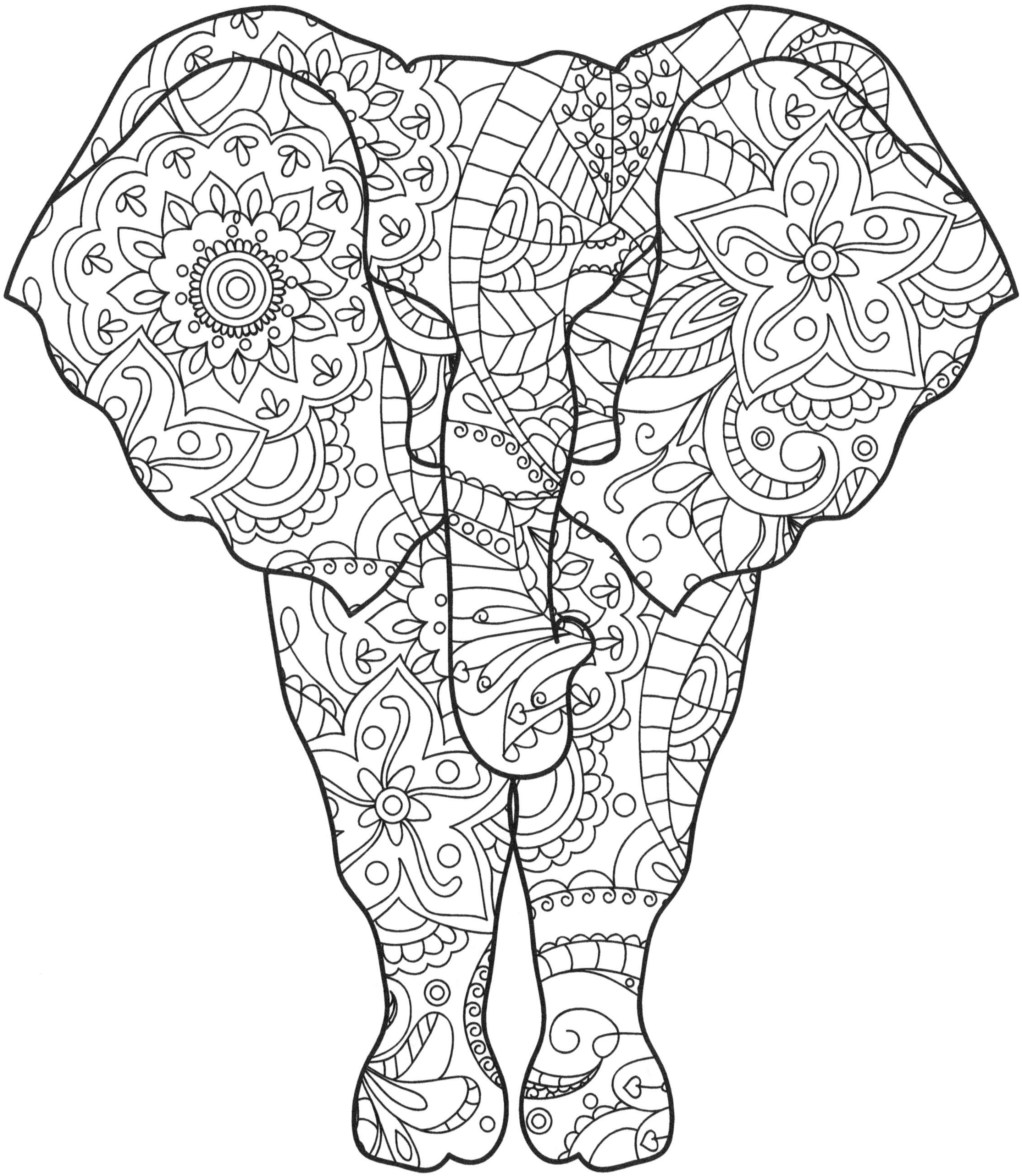

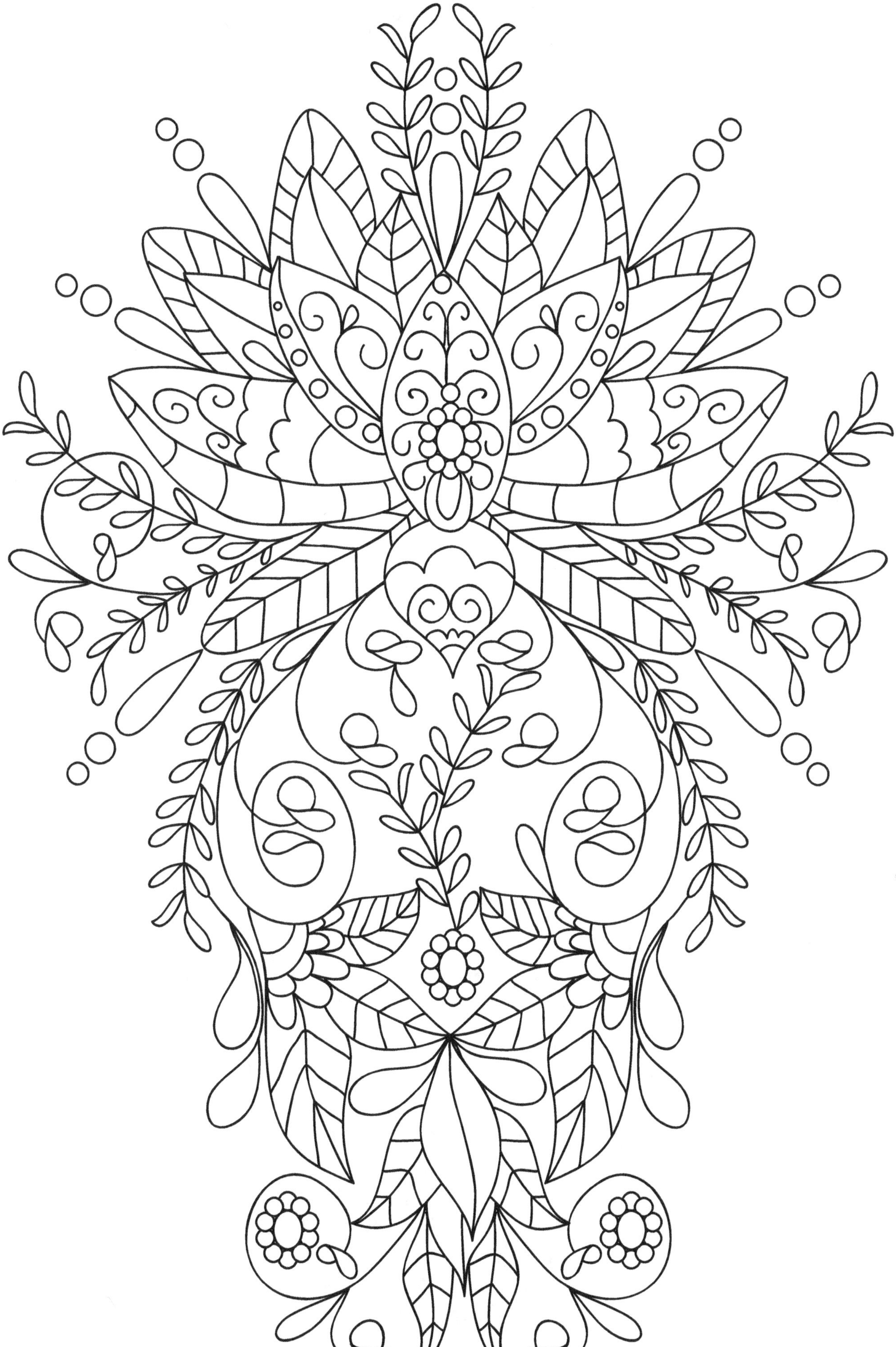

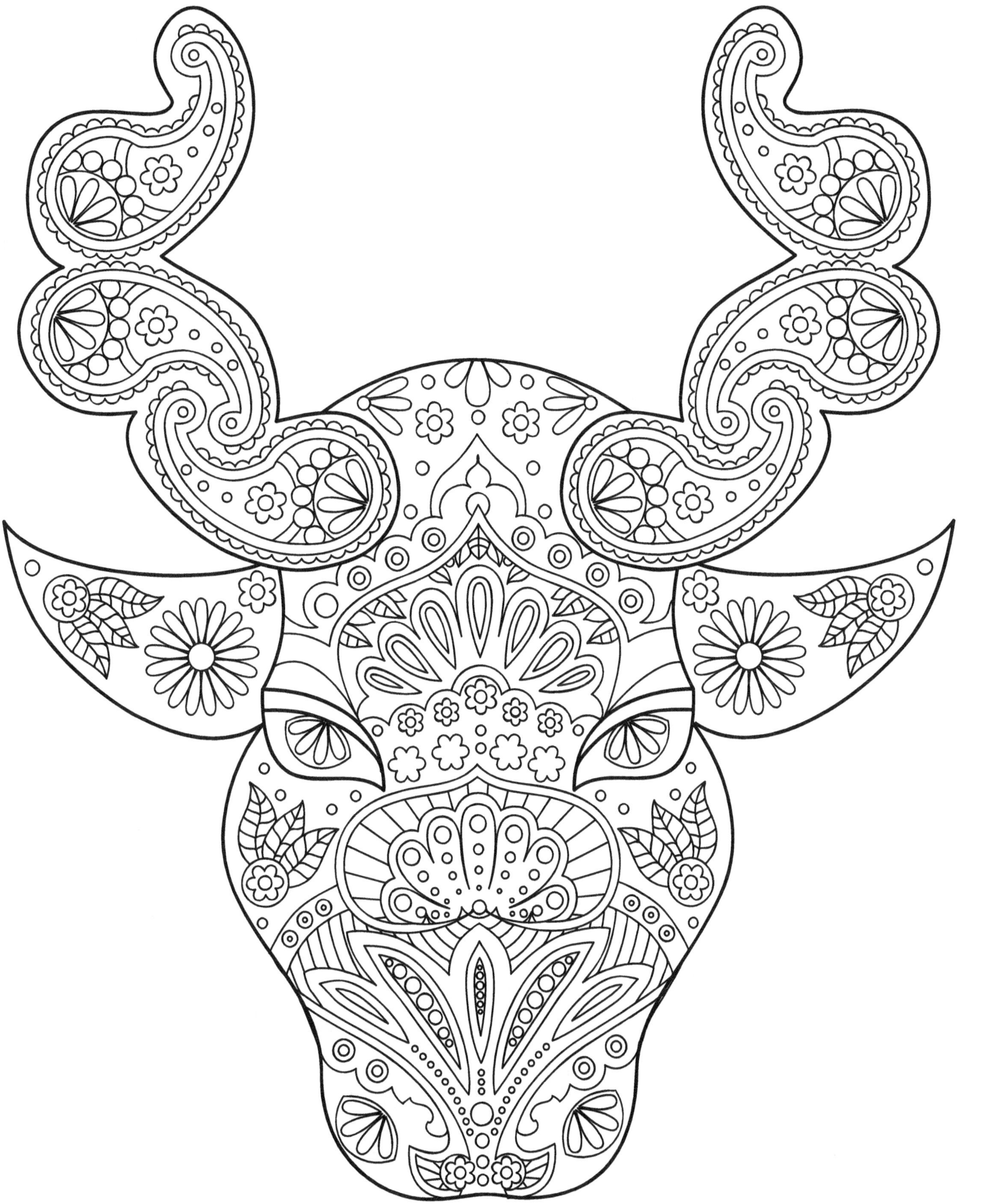

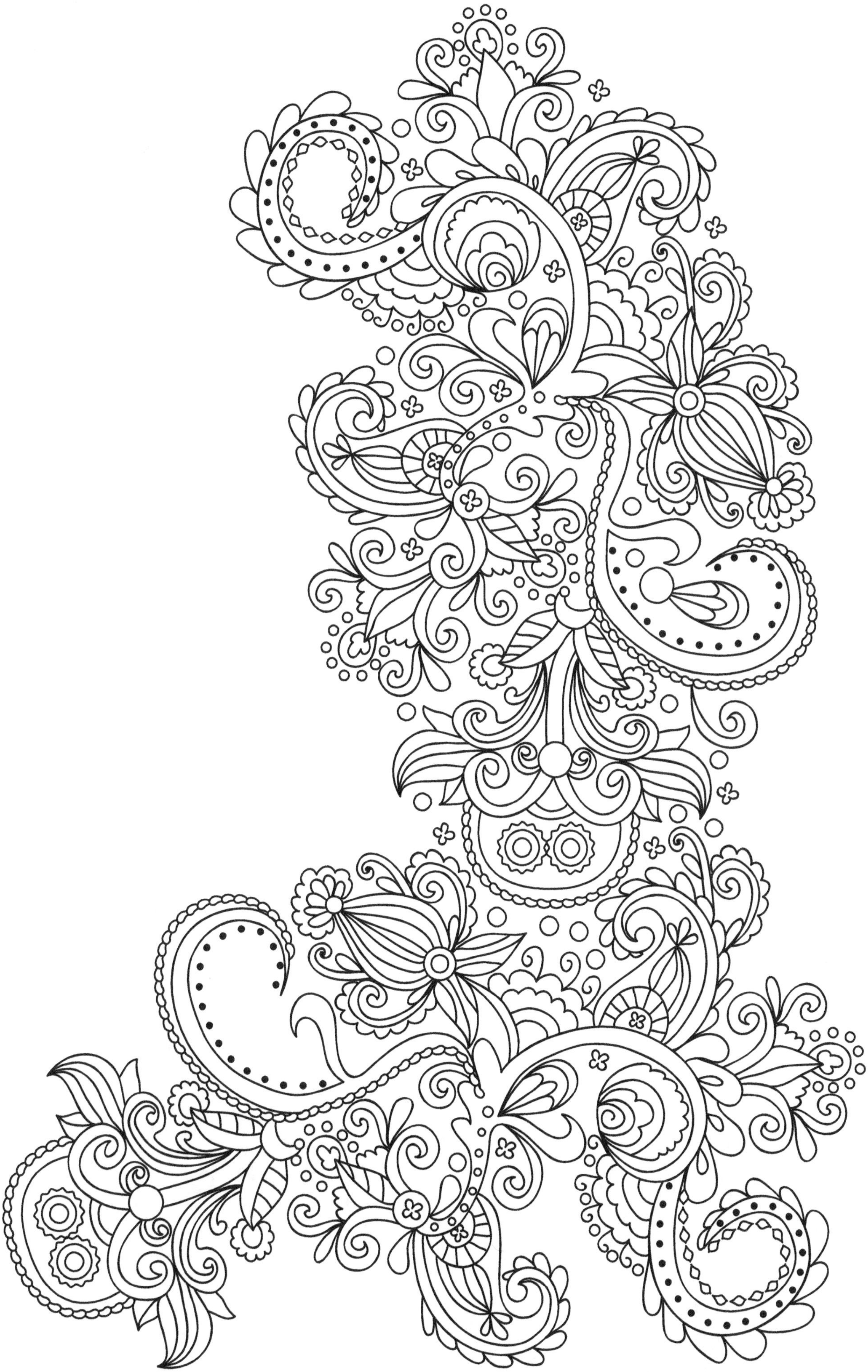

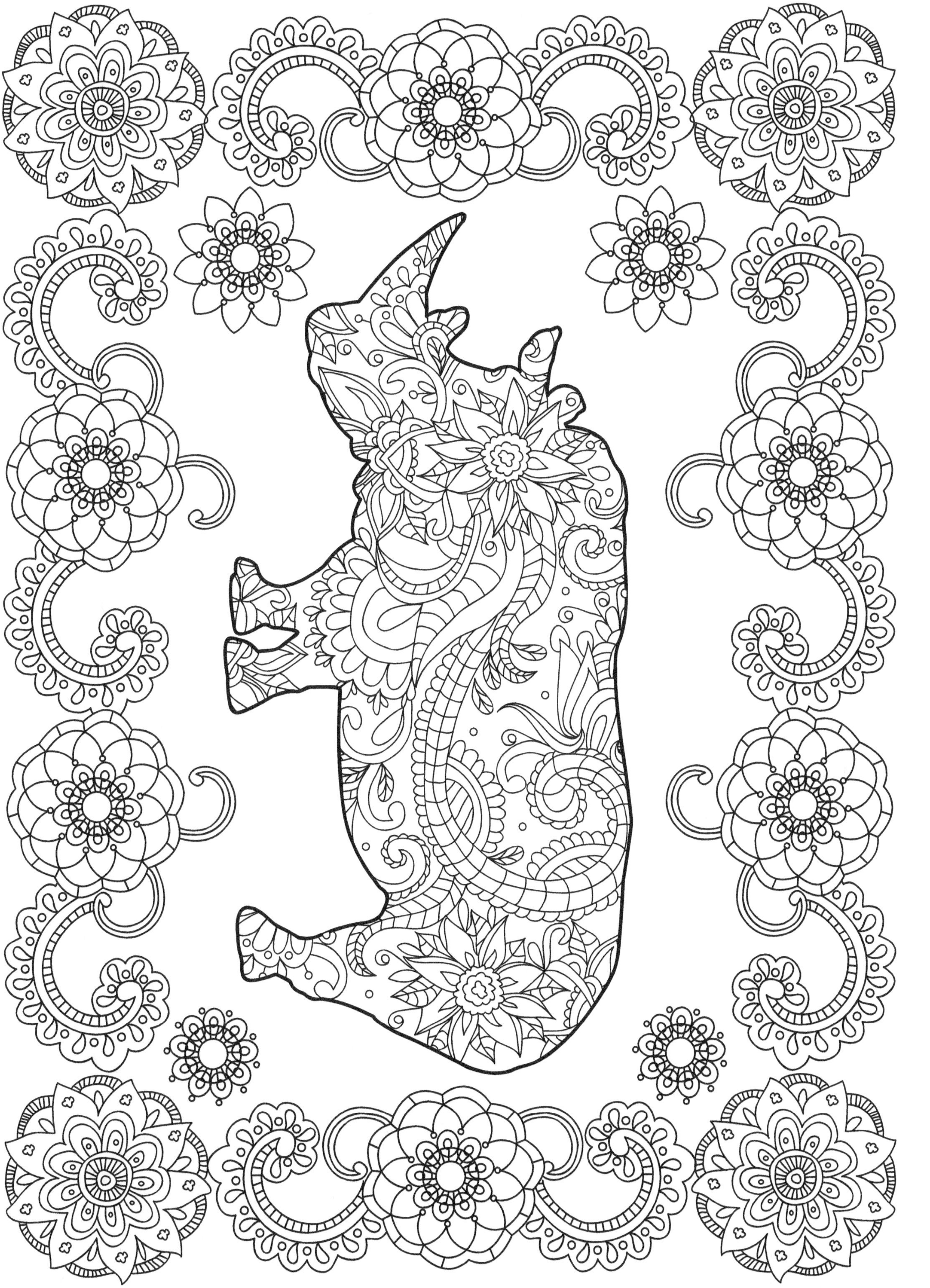

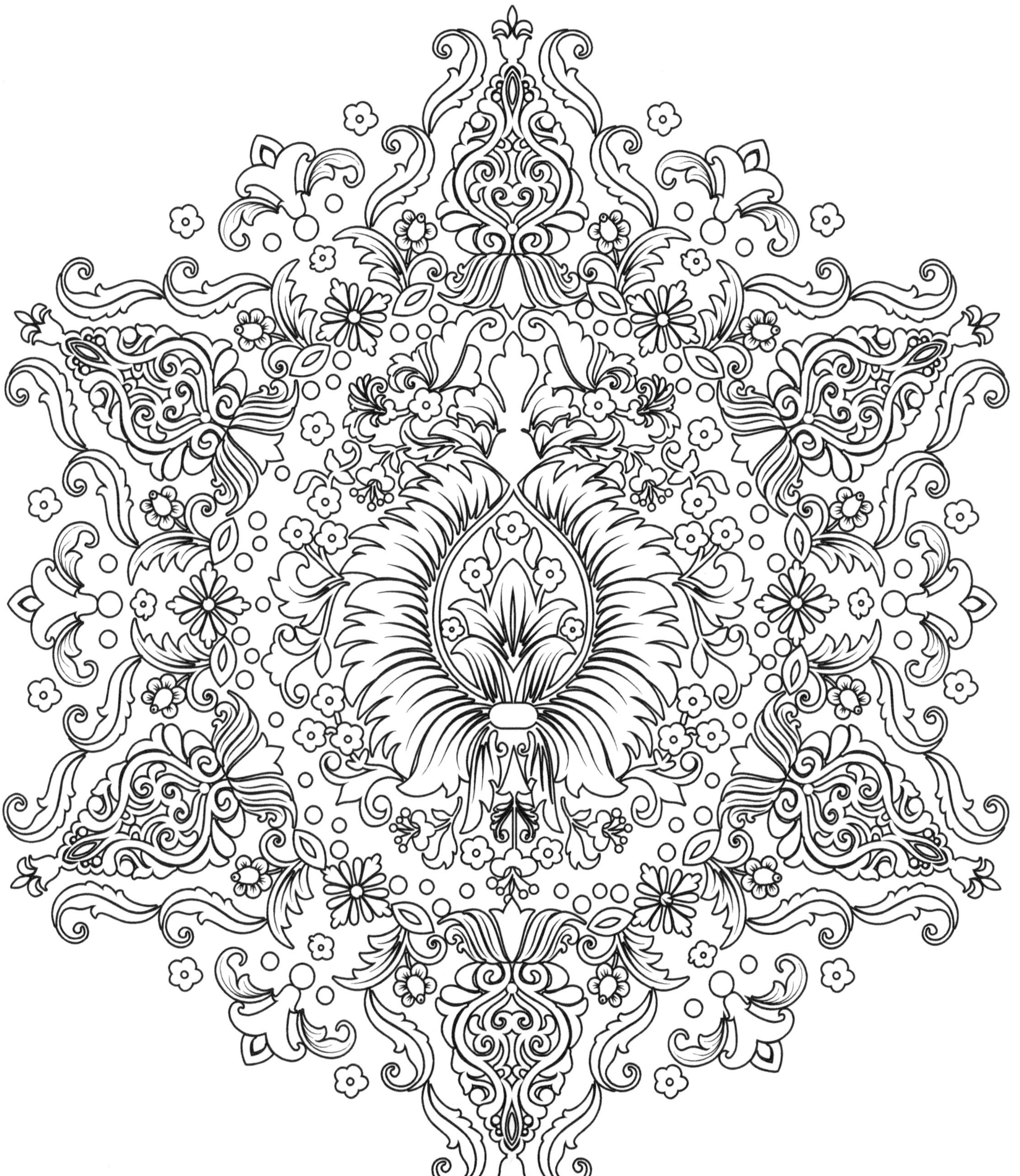

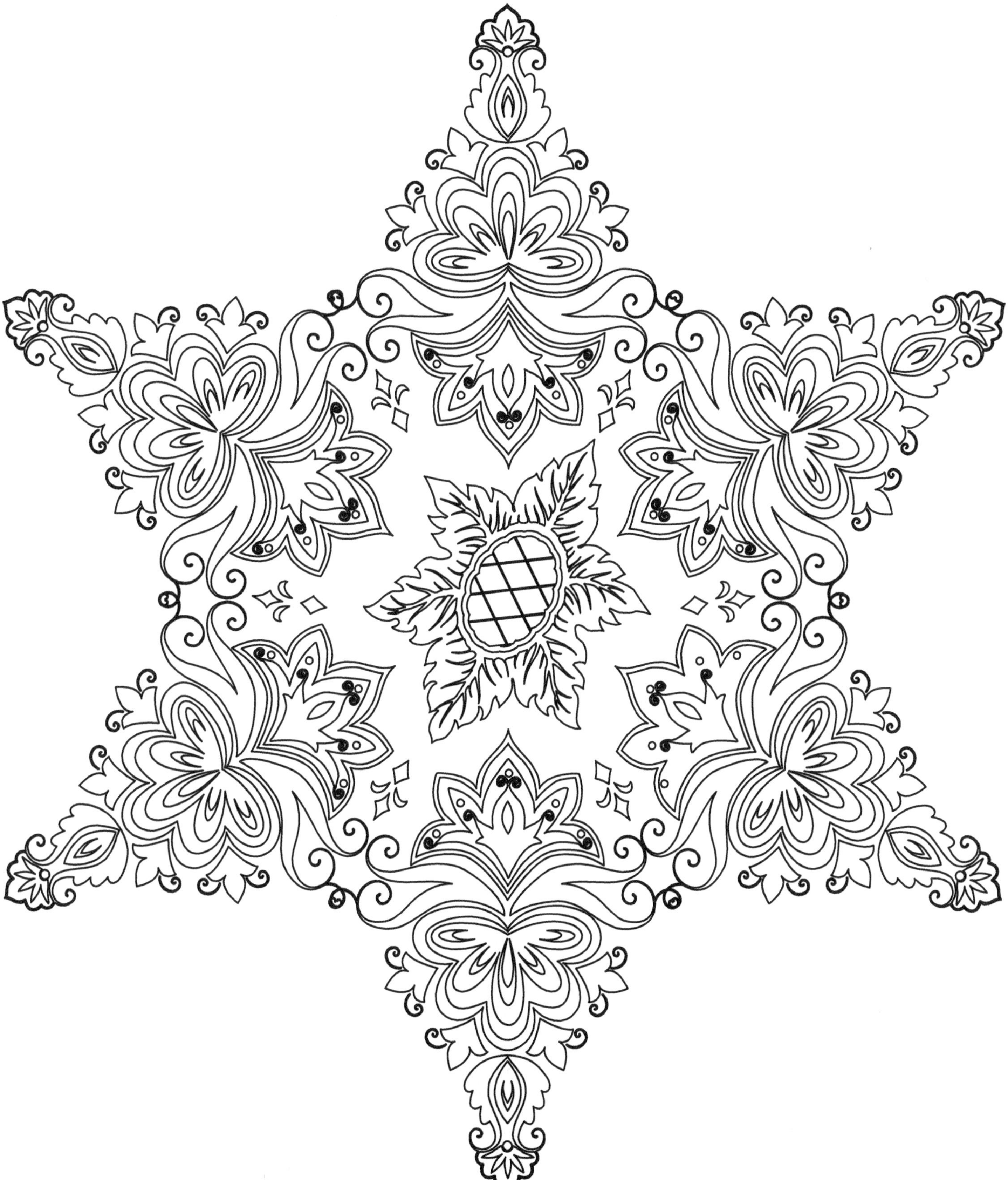

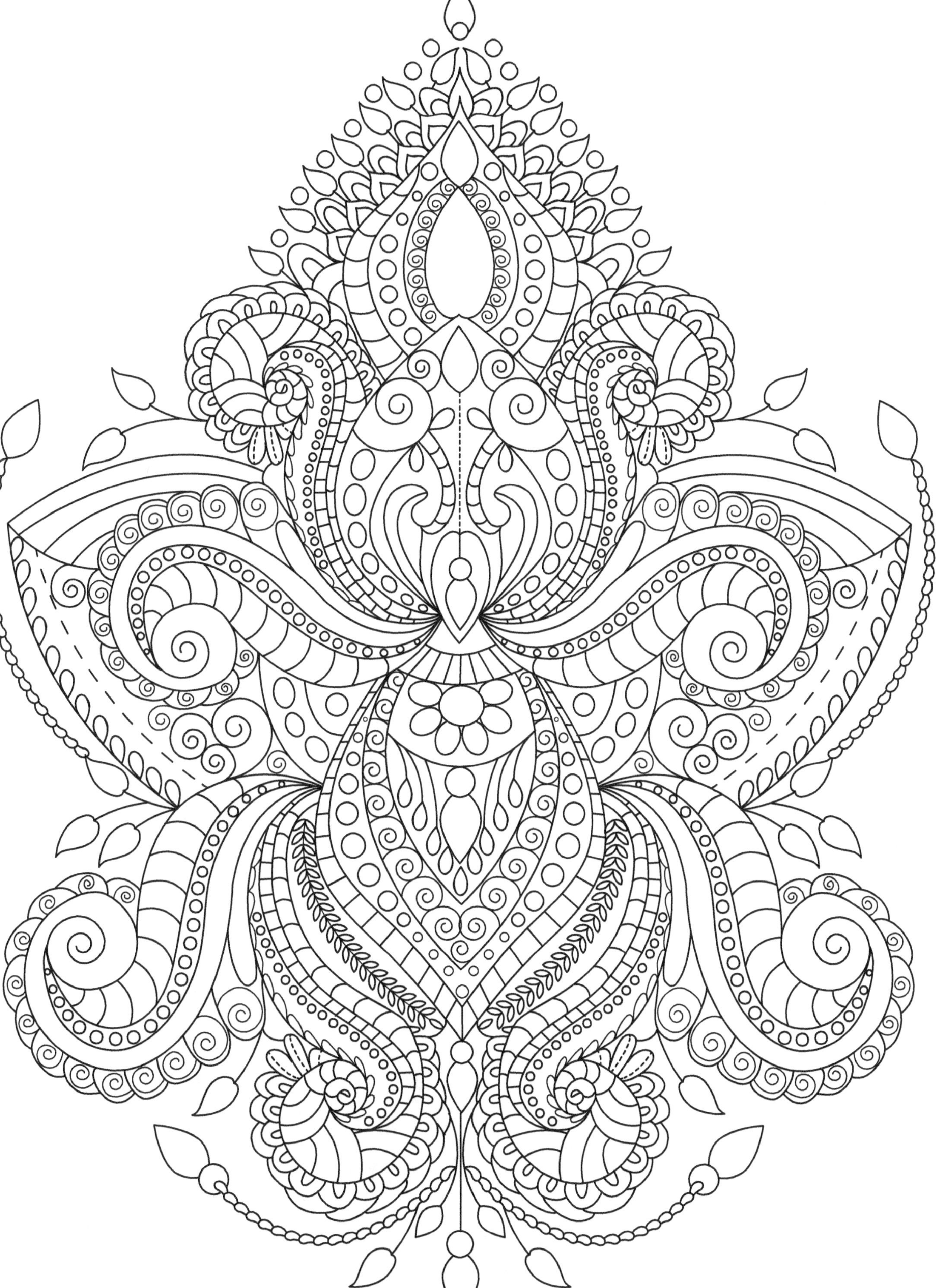

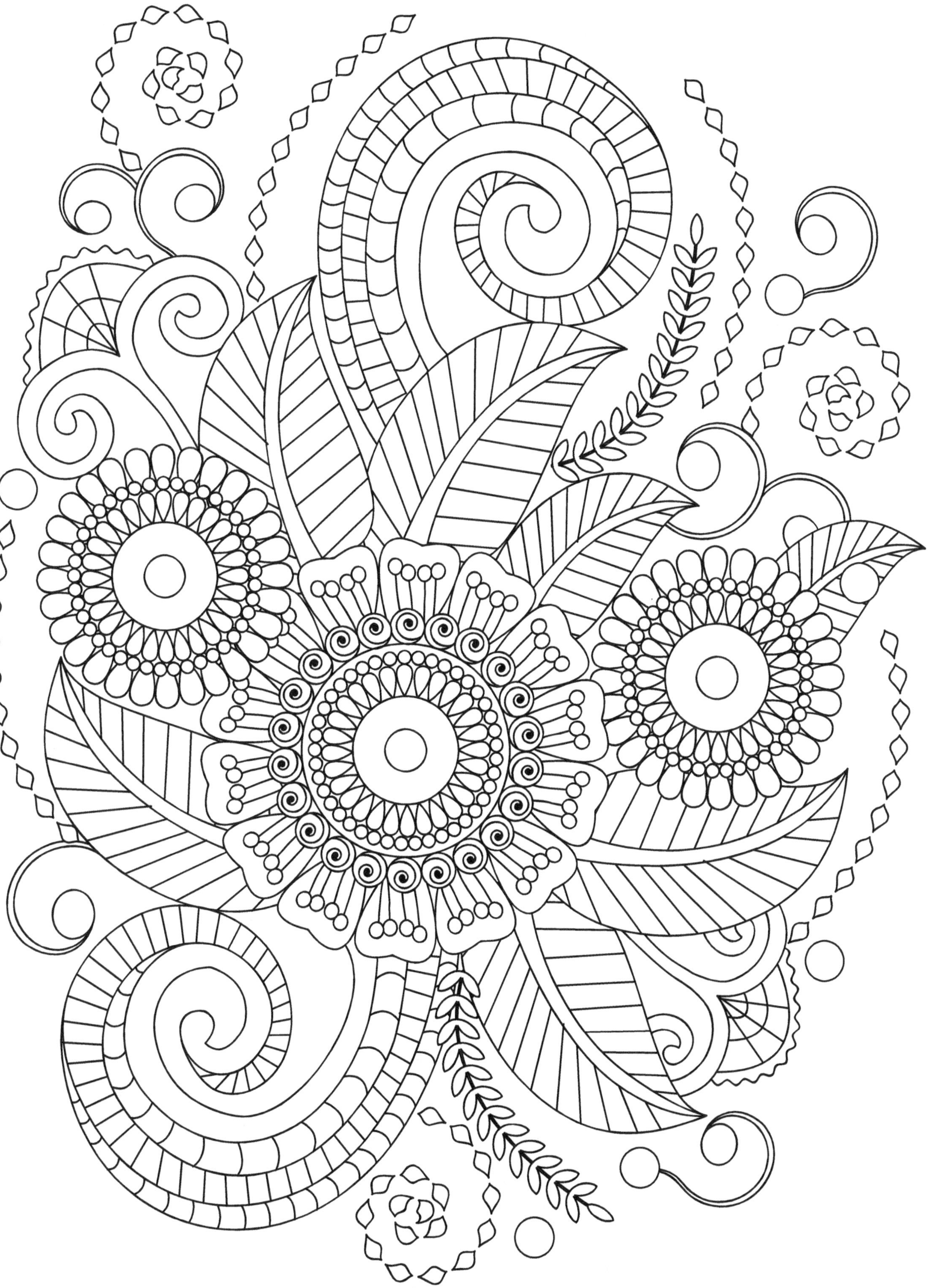

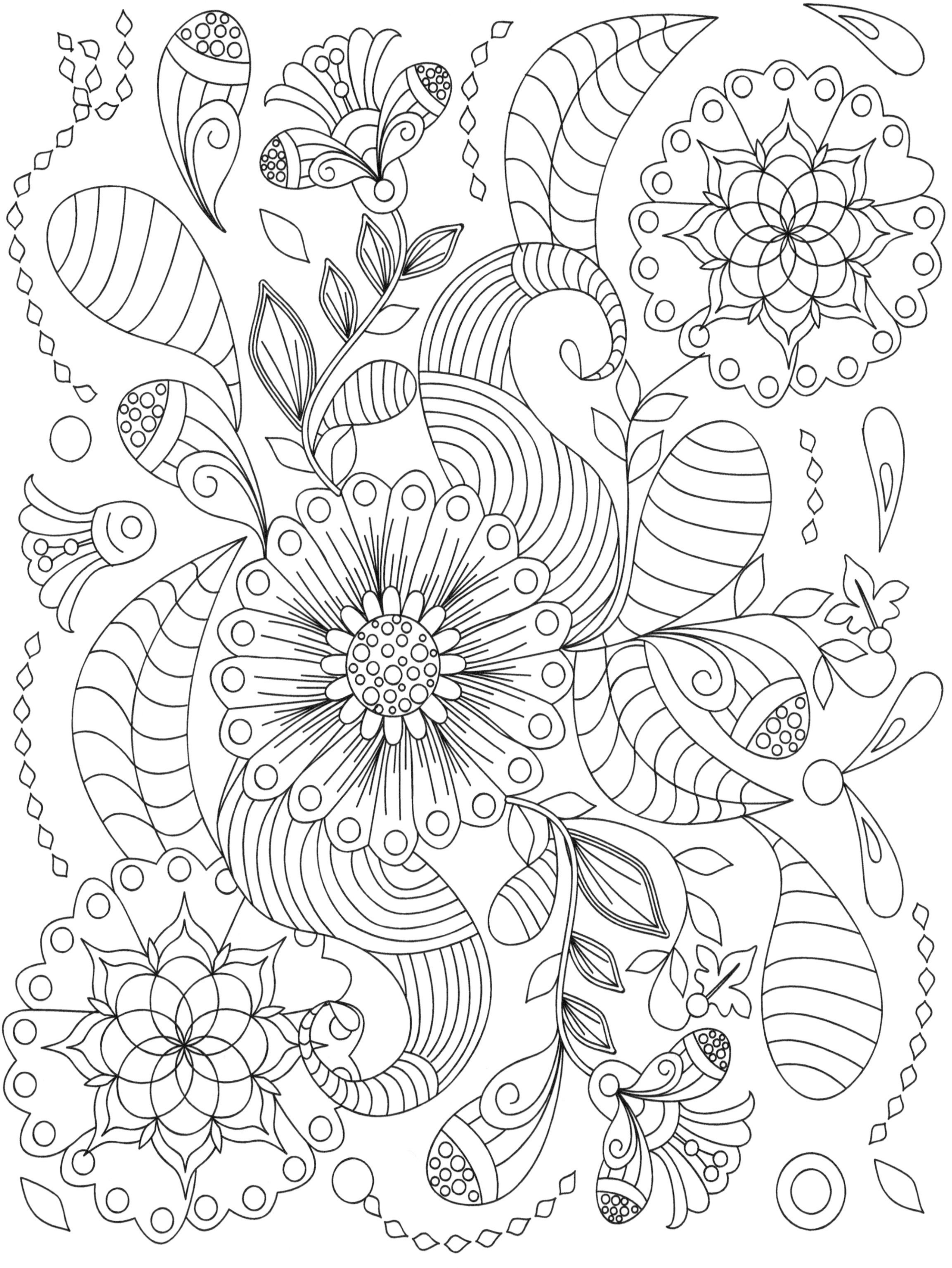

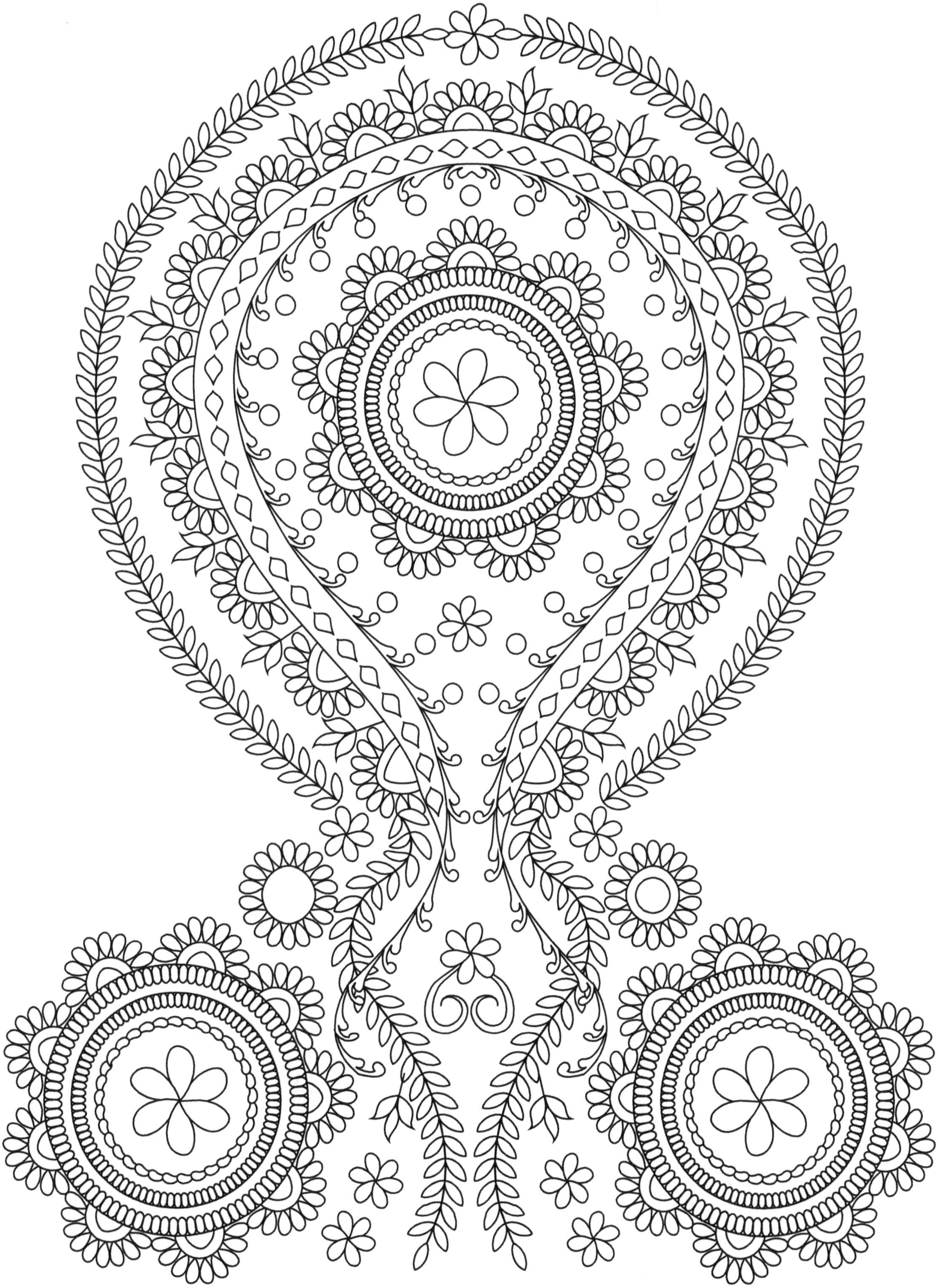

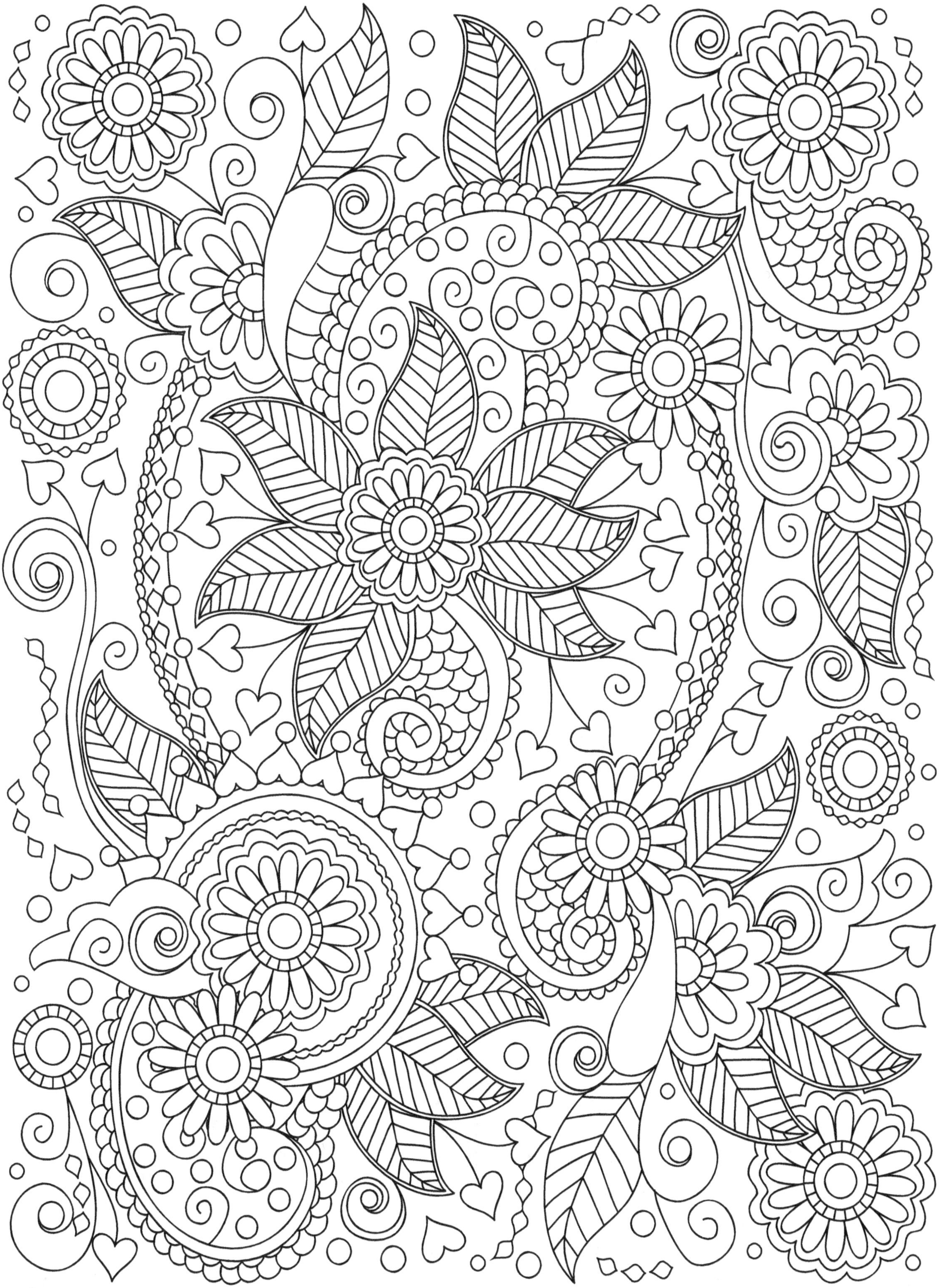

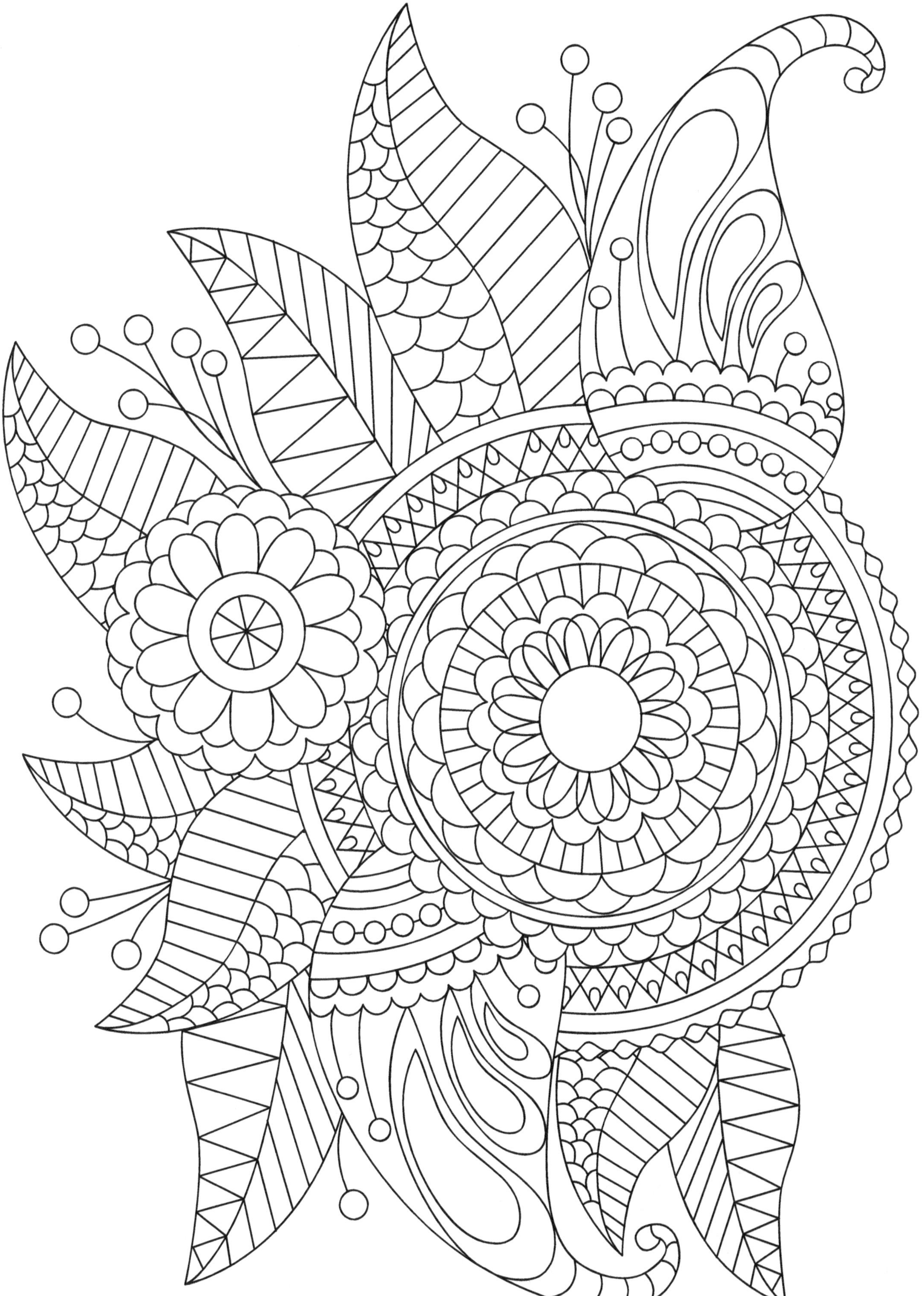